Echoes of
CINCINNATI
REDS
BASEBALL

The Greatest Stories Ever Told

Edited by Mark Stallard

TRIUMPH
BOOKS

Library of Congress Cataloging-in-Publication Data

Echoes of Cincinnati Reds Baseball : the greatest stories ever told / edited by Mark Stallard.
    p. cm.
Includes bibliographical references.
ISBN-13: 978-1-57243-946-7
ISBN-10: 1-57243-946-7
    1. Cincinnati Reds (Baseball team)—History. 2. Baseball—History.
I. Stallard, Mark.

GV875.C65E24 2007
796.3570977178—dc22

                                                2006100449

This book is available in quantity at special discounts for your group or organization. For further information, contact:

Triumph Books
542 South Dearborn Street
Suite 750
Chicago, Illinois 60605
(312) 939-3330
Fax (312) 663-3557

Printed in U.S.A.
ISBN-13: 978-1-57243-946-7
ISBN-10: 1-57243-946-7
Design by Patricia Frey
All photos courtesy of AP/Wide World Photos; cap photo courtesy of Peter Kuehl.

CONTENTS

FOREWORD

I first pitched for the Reds at the end of the 1958 season. After making the team the following spring, I didn't become a regular starter for the club until 1960. Still, I never imagined that just a year later I'd be pitching in the World Series against the New York Yankees.

If you look at the preseason predictions before the 1961 baseball season, the Reds were picked to finish no higher than sixth place in the National League by most of the writers. Throughout the 1950s the Reds had some great hitters: Frank Robinson, Gus Bell, Ted Kluszewski, and Wally Post. Pitching, though, had always been a problem. But in '61 we had what turned out to be a pretty good pitching staff. I won 19 games that season, and I was just starting to get my feet wet when it came to pitching well and winning for the Reds. Our big winner was Joey Jay with 21 wins, and Bob Purkey also had a good season.

Opening Day in Cincinnati has always been special, and back then maybe even more so. The Reds used to play the first game of the season every year because they were the oldest team in baseball, the first professional team. So the Opening Day game at Crosley Field each season had an additional bit of excitement, and to me at least, a real World Series–type atmosphere.

The one thing I always did was work as hard as possible in spring training to win the opening day starting spot. I considered it a tremendous honor to start that first game, kind of a feather in my cap. I took the mound for Cincinnati on Opening Day in 1961 and was fortunate to beat the Cubbies 7–1. I even got a couple of hits.

After we clinched the pennant in late September, our manager, Fred Hutchinson, sent me, Joey Jay, and one of our catchers, Darrell Johnson, to New York to prepare for the World Series against the Yankees. The funny thing about us going there early was that we got to see Roger Maris hit his 61st home run—the shot that broke Babe Ruth's record—off Boston's Tracy Stallard on the last day of the season. I'd never been in Yankee Stadium before, so that was a special moment for me.

Hutch named me to start Game 1 of the Series against the Yankees, and when the game started, I was pretty nervous. The first two hitters I faced reached base, but when I got Maris to pop out, I knew I'd be okay. I settled down and pitched well, but Whitey Ford beat me 2–0 that day. He beat me and the team again in Game 4. That was also the game Ford broke Babe Ruth's pitching record of 29⅔ consecutive scoreless innings in Game 4, a record he eventually stretched to 33 innings.

In a week's time, I saw two of the Babe's greatest records broken.

I wish we would have played better than we did in that Series, but the Yankees had an incredible ball club. Purkey pitched great in Game 3 and ended up taking a tough loss when Maris homered in the ninth inning. We didn't win the Series, but that doesn't take anything away from that season. It had been 21 years since the Reds had won a pennant and that was much too long for the city and her fans.

Cincinnati became my home—it's a great city, a great place to raise a family, and with 11 kids and 31 grandchildren, that was important to me. How important was the 1961 season to me? I used the money I got from the World Series to buy the house I still live in.

Every time I put the on Reds uniform I tried to appreciate the significance of the team and remember how important it is to the fans. And it's the history of the team that is conveyed on the pages of this book—the great players, managers, and games that have made the Reds the unique organization that it is. The articles and stories in this book convey the wonderful history of the Reds organization.

—Jim O'Toole

INTRODUCTION

When baseball began its quick ascent into the national psyche of the American public, the words of the first sportswriters firmly placed a lasting imprint of the game on the fans' minds. Things have changed a great deal since those first scribes jotted down and published their thoughts and insights on baseball, especially the language used and the way games are reported. Today we can jump to a website and read a complete summary of a game less than an hour after it ends. No matter where you might live in the world, complete coverage is just a click away.

It wasn't always this easy.

In major league cities at the turn of the 20th century, especially New York and Chicago, there were so many newspapers available that fans could buy five different publications and literally get five distinctive versions of the same game. On a national level, baseball fans waited impatiently for their copies of *The Sporting News (TSN)* and *Baseball Magazine* to arrive, hoping to find an article about their favorite team or player. Other national publications, such as the *Saturday Evening Post* and *Esquire*, occasionally had baseball articles, but *TSN* and *Baseball Magazine* ruled the national baseball scene.

In Cincinnati, fans could choose from the *Times-Star*, the *Enquirer*, or the *Post* to read about their beloved Reds. Writers such as James Isaminger, Stanley Frank, Lou Smith, Jack Cronin, Earl Lawson, and, most recently, John Erardi, covered the Reds for the local press. On a national level, F.C. Lane and W.A. Phelon wrote about the game for *Baseball Magazine*. Other great writers, like George Vecsey and Roger Kahn, wrote for several publications. Ron Fimrite and Steve Wulf wrote excellent baseball stories for *Sports Illustrated*.

Every memorable Reds moment, player, or manager has been written about, in one form or another, which presented a gigantic problem when compiling this book. How could I effectively pare down 125 years of Reds history into a couple hundred pages? What players to select or leave out, and what great moments do I make sure are included? It wasn't an easy task.

The Reds' history is rich with Hall-of-Fame players. From Heine Groh to Ken Griffey Jr., the club had standout players every decade of the 20th century and one of the greatest teams of all time in the 1970s.

viii   ECHOES OF CINCINNATI REDS BASEBALL

On the flip side, the Reds were involved—indirectly both times—in the two greatest scandals in major league history: the Black Sox's throwing of the 1919 World Series and the sad saga of Pete Rose's banishment from the game for gambling. I tried to select a full representation of the team's entire history.

This collection of previously published stories on the Cincinnati Reds was gathered from many different sources: *Baseball Magazine, The Sporting News, Sports Illustrated, SPORT, The Saturday Evening Post*, and newspapers in Cincinnati, New York, and Chicago. The best thing about this collection is the time stamp almost every piece has: 1940 World Series coverage, Johnny Vander Meer's second no-hitter, and Pete Rose's 44-game hitting streak.

The words of the day.

Reading these tales transports you to the moment they happened, allowing you to relive the same joy or heartbreak as the readers of that era. You'll experience Reds baseball through the hearts and minds of the writers who loved the game as much as you do today.

I hope you enjoy this special look at Reds history.

—Mark Stallard

Echoes of
CINCINNATI
REDS
BASEBALL

Eppa Rixey is one of baseball's best all-time left-handed pitchers, and one of the greatest characters the game has seen over the years.

Section I
THE PLAYERS

New York World

TWENTY YEARS A PLAYER

One of the first great players to don a Reds uniform, Bid McPhee spent all 18 years of his major league career with Cincinnati. Only four other players have played more games as a second-sacker than "King Bid," who was considered the best second baseman of the 19th century. Elected to the Hall of Fame in 2000, McPhee led his league in double plays 11 times and posted the best fielding average in nine seasons. In 1987, the New York World ran this profile article about the great second baseman.

John Alexander McPhee, or "Biddy," as he is familiarly called, the second baseman of the Cincinnati Reds, is a record-breaker in the tenure of service on the diamond, as well as in his standing for playing. His engagement for this season makes 20 years that he has been regularly engaged in the sport. He has outserved several generations of players, and has played with all of the leading baseballists of his time.

He was born in Massena, New York, November 1, 1859. His father was a Scotchman, and his mother came from a prominent Yankee family of Puritan stock. John T. Brush, president of the Cincinnati club, was also born in Massena, New York. Although about the same age, Brush and McPhee never knew each other until Brush became the owner of the Cincinnati club.

He has had many chances to go to other clubs, but his many friends in Cincinnati and his great liking for the city of his adoption keep him here. He is a great home favorite and has been the recipient of many presents from admiring friends in this city.

A few days ago action was taken by McPhee's local admirers for the purpose of presenting him a substantial testimonial in recognition of his long and faithful service with the Cincinnati team.

Testimonial to McPhee

Subscriptions to this are now pouring in. The Chamber of Commerce, W.W. Peabody, vice president of the B.O. & S.W. RR; Samuel Bailey, former United States Sub-Treasurer, and many other prominent persons are taking an active part in the affair. Substantial, indeed, will be the testimonial, as rumor has it that a house and lot will be presented to him.

For many years McPhee was recognized as the only player in the league playing an infield position who did not use a glove. It has been in the last season or two only that he resorted to the use of a glove, which was brought about by an injury to his left hand that left that member tender.

While he has been for many years looked upon as the "King" second baseman, he is so graceful and accurate in his position that many plays from McPhee are not called great because his action is quiet and unassuming and the baseball public has become used to them.

When McPhee was seven years old his family removed to Kaithsburg, a small hamlet of 1,700 inhabitants in western Illinois, where Park Wilson, the great backstop of the New York club, was born and reared. Wilson's father was running a dry-goods store in the town, and McPhee was for some time a clerk and an all-around helper in the store. Both Wilson and McPhee played with a local team called the Ictorias. They were called by the fans the "fly-catchers."

The team sent East for uniforms and played all the clubs of the surrounding towns, being a leading feature for the county fairs at that time. This club won the first prize in the district league. The prize was a nickel-plated bat. McPhee was at that time playing behind the bat, and was a good catcher. He was the youngest player in the team, being only 16 years of age. In 1877 he and Elmer Rockwell were signed by the club at Davenport, Iowa, and they constituted what was then known as a crack battery, with Rockwell in the box and McPhee behind the bat.

In the Davenport club McPhee also played second base and in the right field in 1878. In 1879 McPhee did not play ball, but secured a position as clerk in a commission house in Davenport. In the spring of 1880 he went to Akron, Ohio, and played second base in the semi-league club that played the Cleveland club on off days.

In the autumn of 1880 O.P. Caylor formed the American Association and sent Charlie Jones, the old left fielder of the Reds, to Akron, to sign McPhee, Sam Wise, and Kemmler, the two latter being now out of the business, while McPhee is still playing with Cincinnati. McPhee lives in this city with his parents, who have resided here since 1884. He is a man of excellent habits, always takes good care of himself, smokes and drinks very little, and spends most of his time at home.

McPhee on How to Play

When asked how to play second base, McPhee said he played it no different than anyone else. He said that a good shortstop is a great help to the second baseman, and when the two understand each other well they can cover much more ground and do it safely.

Of course, there is much depending on all members of the team playing well together, but no two men, not even the batteries, can mutually help each other more than the second baseman and the shortstop. McPhee said when he was playing ball he always tried to avoid accidents. While he always wanted to win, yet he would prefer to be credited with an error than with an injury, and for that reason he has only been out of the game on account of disabilities for three weeks during his long career of 20 years.

He says the batters are getting things down so fine now that they can fool all the fielders, usually hitting the ball as they please and driving it where least expected—formerly the fielders would take certain positions for the right-handed men and other positions for the left-handed men, but now there is no such thing as catching the batter by shifting around in this manner. There was also much interest in studying certain batters who were known to drive the ball in given directions, but now the batter hits to dodge the fielders, and this part of the sport is almost down to a fine art, so much so that the fielders are unable to keep up with it.

McPhee has held the second-base record off and on for many years and is without doubt at the head of the list on the average. While he is considered one of the best men that ever covered second base, he also stands high as a good batter and a man who attends strictly to his business in the general interest of his team.

McPhee is bright and a good talker. He stands well in his own community.

Baseball Magazine

FOUR HUNDRED TO ONE

The man who made the "bottle bat" famous, or maybe it was the other way around. Heine Groh's lumber had a nontapered barrel with a thin handle, and he batted with a wide-open stance that allowed him to drop bunts or slap the ball to the opposite field. The Reds' third baseman for nine seasons, Groh was a member of the 1919 world champions. The September 1915 issue of Baseball Magazine *profiled Groh's hitting technique.*

How should a big-league player stand at bat? When a single player uses one system and four hundred of his mates use quite another, the chances seem to be overwhelmingly in favor of the four hundred. But the arguments brought out by Heine Groh in explanation of his unique method are surely plausible, while the arguments in favor of the prevailing type are by no means so convincing. There must be some best way to stand at bat. And if the present way isn't the best, why not have a change?

When Pop Anson used to bat, he grasped the bludgeon firmly, faced the pitcher with his feet squarely on the ground, and as the ball whirled from the pitcher's hand he stepped forward to meet it. Evidence goes to show that a good many old timers followed the same system of facing the pitcher with a resolute, steadfast gaze and a steady hand. Why is it that as baseball progressed the batter turned more and more from his head-on attitude until he finally stood with his side toward the pitcher and had to crane his neck if he would see the ball? Was it an improvement on the old style?

We believe no one knows why batters stand as they do when they take their position at the plate. No two of them stand exactly alike. But there is a wide difference between the type of Pop Anson and any assumed by modern big-league batters.

Did we say any? No, there is one exception, for Heine Groh, of Cincinnati, is the sole survivor in the big leagues of an old tradition immortalized by Pop Anson. Groh alone stands facing the pitcher instead of sideways. And Groh steps forward to meet the ball just as the old timers used to do.

Any batting example set by Pop Anson is good enough for someone to follow, for Anson was one of the three or four greatest batters in the records of the game. For the matter of that, Groh himself is a batter of no mean proclivities and it has puzzled many people to know why it was that McGraw made his famous trade with Joe Tinker to get Fromme. Fromme has gone but Ames still pitches apparently as well as he ever did. And Groh, thrown in for good measure, is one of the best infielders in the league. McGraw couldn't use him at second base, his rightful position, because he had Larry Doyle. But Groh outbatted Larry all last season and fielded much the better of the two. Still, that's beside the story.

Groh gives a very plausible argument in favor of his own peculiar method. He says, "By standing facing the pitcher, you can see both foul lines, watch the pitcher's windup motion better, and follow the ball better. These things are very important. In addition, by standing in that way, the batter unconsciously steps forward to meet the ball. When he swings, the force of the swing itself carries him toward first base and really gets him into his stride. I have always batted in that way, although sometimes I have been told that I should change my system. I know Kinsella told me I had better try the ordinary style of batting when I first signed with the Giants. The only reason he gave for this was that I was liable to get hit in the head standing as I did. It never seemed to me that there was any likelihood of this. I should think a man would be better able to dodge a pitched ball by facing it than he could by standing with his side toward it, for in facing it he could twist with equal ease to either side. Some players have told me that they shouldn't think I could hit the ball very hard meeting it in that way. You don't have to hit the ball very hard to drive it safe, and the records will show that I have made quite a few extra-base hits."

What Groh says is substantially correct. Last year he batted .288, which is very good for an infielder. Furthermore, he made 18 doubles, four triples, and two home runs.

Oddly enough on the very day that I talked to Groh he went into the game and knocked out two two-base hits. Both were vicious drives that traveled fast and far. They were a clinching argument against the fallacy that the batter who meets the ball fair cannot hit it hard.

Tommy Leach, fellow teammate of Groh's, and a veteran of many years' experience, related the following, "Groh came to me early in the season and asked me if I thought he ought to try to change his style. He said that some persons were criticizing him and wondered if he might do better by standing in the regulation way. I told him to pay no attention to such remarks, that every batter had his individual style and that his was well adapted to his own peculiar needs. There are a good many arguments in favor of Groh's style. There is no doubt the batter in such a position can see the ball better and follow the foul lines better. The only objection that I would be inclined to say is that the batter is likely to hit late and so drive the ball to right field, but most batters have the tendency to hit either into one field or another, so that that handicap isn't as great as it seems."

Jake Daubert, who has led the league two years in batting, claims that he once used Groh's system. "I was in the minor leagues at the time," says Jake, "and it seemed natural for me to face the pitcher. I always thought there were good arguments in favor of that style, but as I was a weak hitter at the time, I changed over and finally got going pretty well at the regulation way. No doubt if I had been able to hit at first, I would have stuck to that system, as I probably wouldn't have hit well at that stage of the game under any circumstances."

Zack Wheat's principal objection to the attitude of Groh at the bat is this, "I don't think I could swing well at the ball standing that way. I generally swing from the handle of the bat. I don't think any one who does swing for extra-base hits could use that system, but for the man who chops at the ball and chokes up on the bat, I should think it would be just about right."

Hans Wagner doesn't say much, generally, but he was rather interested in the intimation that almost all big-league batters were not using the best style. "Pop Anson used to bat that way, sure enough," said Wagner, "and it looks like good dope. I don't bat that way myself, and I don't just know why. I guess it didn't come natural to me, that's all."

Wagner's argument seems to be the prevailing one among ballplayers. They don't bat that way because it doesn't come natural, or, in other words, because they have been used to seeing everyone else bat in the ordinary style. But it doesn't come natural to a right-handed man to bat left-handed and there are a great many other things about baseball that players have learned and in which they now excel that didn't come natural at first.

To an outsider, the man who sits in the stand, it does look rather strange to see a player stand up with his side toward the pitcher like a crab, and crane his neck around in order to get a view of the ball. Instead of being a natural position, it looks very unnatural.

Jimmy Archer, the famous Cubs backstop, however, was a firm adherent of the modern method. He said, "Groh almost always hits toward right field. That is because, standing as he does, he swings a trifle late. There are advantages to his system, he gets into his stride easier, but the managers never try to teach a player how to hit. They know that every man must hit in his own way, if at all."

All this is true, no doubt, but what Archer says of the managers hardly applies. It would be foolish to try to get Ty Cobb or Tris Speaker or any one of the veteran sluggers to change their manner of swinging at the bat, but the managers have made many more radical changes in their recruit players than this change would necessitate, and if there is any merit in the idea, as seems to be the case, it would be to the managers' advantage to encourage the Groh style of batting among their younger players.

For, after all is said and done, the main argument in favor of the prevailing style is no argument at all. The batter stands as he does simply because everybody else stands that way, and he has always been accustomed to the type from the days of his infancy. It has probably, in most cases, never even occurred to him that there might be a better way, and the managers apparently have given no thought to the subject either.

If there is merit in the idea, which seems to be the case at first blush, its general adoption might conceivably revolutionize the entire science of batting, exempting the sluggers, who would object to the system because it curtails the length of their swing. It might prove an advantage to the rank and file, the players who are inclined to chop at the ball. In any case, the idea seems to have been most fruitful of success in certain striking cases and deserves far more consideration than it has apparently received.

For Groh's argument seems unanswerable. "You can see the ball better with two eyes than you can with an eye and a half. For that is about all you really use when you twist your neck to get a sight of the ball."

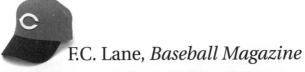

F.C. Lane, *Baseball Magazine*

EPPA, NOT JEPTHA, RIXEY—A COLORFUL SOUTHPAW

The winningest left-hander in baseball prior to Warren Spahn, Eppa Rixey also ranks seventh in all-time losses. He had a good fastball, curve, and change of pace in his repertoire of pitches and took the mound for the final 13 seasons of his long career for the Reds. Tall and lanky, Rixey used a "pretzel" windup and is one of the few major leaguers to have never played in a minor league game. F.C. Lane authored this article on Rixey for the February 1930 issue of Baseball Magazine.

Far down in the second division finished the Cincinnati Reds. But that was no fault of Eppa Rixey, who is still going strong after 17 consecutive seasons of big-league hurling. And this amazing southpaw is still a fine pitcher

One of the most interesting players in the major leagues is Eppa Rixey. The gentleman from Culpeper, Virginia, has completed 17 seasons of continuous service as a National League pitcher. If he survives until the third day of May, next spring, he will be 38 years of age, and his prospects as a life insurance risk are excellent. Incidentally, Rixey sells insurance in the off-season, so he can tell you all about it.

How many pitchers have worked for 17 seasons in the big leagues? How many are going strong in their 38th year? The number isn't impressive, never was and never will be. For pitching is a strenuous occupation and few survive the wear and tear of 17 seasons and are as well preserved as this eccentric but likeable Southerner.

Rixey is a gentleman of the Old Dominion State. He developed a flair for chemistry and holds a master's degree from the University of Virginia. To him, that knightly character, Robert E. Lee, is a living reality, and he fairly oozes romantic stories of the great Civil War. For all that, he is a cosmopolitan soul and finds life among the "damned Yankees" (he resides in Cincinnati) not so irksome as one might suppose. As Mrs. Rixey's people hail from Vermont, her husband, doubtless, finds it advisable to temper his strong southern prejudices, although opposing ballplayers can always get his goat by whistling "Marching through Georgia."

The demoralizing influences of northern associations upon a gentleman born below the Mason and Dixon Line were called in question by a Cincinnati teammate who accused Rixey of voting the Republican ticket in the recent presidential election. To this base charge Rixey responded, "A gentleman in the South votes the Democratic ticket. In the North a gentleman," and here he looked hesitatingly up and down the bench, "seems to vote the Republican ticket. Wherever I am, I try to be a gentleman." And with that dignified, if somewhat cryptic rejoinder, the discussion terminated.

Rixey's excellent work, at an age when most pitchers have long since faded from the public view, cannot be laid to a specially easy type of pitching. Grover Alexander, for example, has lasted so long because his pitching style is designedly easy upon the arm. Alexander always puts the first ball over and follows by putting most of the others over. The batter swings or strikes out, to suit his own convenience. And swinging, he either speedily hits or is retired. Hence, Alexander pitches fewer balls in a given contest than any other hurler.

Rixey, on the contrary, pitches a lot of balls. One hundred and twenty or one hundred and thirty in nine innings is a very fair showing for him. Last summer, while discussing ways and means of saving the "old soup bone," I casually mentioned to Rixey that he pitched an unnecessarily great number of balls during a game; that if he put the first one over, a la Alexander, he would save himself some unnecessary work.

Rixey was impressed by the logic of the case. "My arm is beginning to squeak a little," he said. "Maybe I could cut down on the number of pitches."

That afternoon was Rixey's allotted appointment upon the hurling mound. Sure enough, batter after batter saw the first ball cut the plate. He got through the first inning with eight pitched balls, the second with seven. But in the third came an avalanche of base hits. The ball shot to all corners of the field, sharp, zipping singles. Through this barrage might presently be seen the dejected figure of Brother Eppa headed for the bench and the showers.

Next morning I saw him leaning against the wall at the door of his hotel. When he noticed me, he turned his back at first, then slowly revolving, greeted me with a withering glance from his 6'6" of impressive attitude. Meanwhile, I tried to look as sorrowful as the situation seemed to demand. Twice he opened his mouth to speak, but words failed him. A vision of that lost game, that ignominious retreat was still too fresh in his memory. He sighed, "That was a hell of a system," he said.

But resentment, even righteous indignation is foreign to Rixey's genial nature. Presently he became modified and discussed the situation with his usual keen insight into baseball things.

"A pitcher is foolish," he says, "to follow anybody else's style. No two pitchers are alike. What's good for one is bad dope for another. I'm too old a dog to be learning new tricks. I should have known better.

"It is true I pitch a lot of balls. But generally I don't bear down very hard on more than half a dozen during a game. I like to work on a batter. My control has always been pretty good. I know I can get the ball over if I want to, but I scheme to make the batter hit at a bad ball. I rather like to go down the line, that is three balls and two strikes. It doesn't bother me a bit and it's not an indication of wildness either. It's just my style."

Queried upon his durable qualities, Rixey remarked, "Some ballplayers seem to wear well. This is quite apart from physical strength. Hack Miller was probably the strongest man, physically, that ever played baseball. He could bend iron bars and pull up small trees by the roots. For all that, he didn't last every long. Everett Scott was as slim as a string bean. You might have thought he would break an ankle sliding bases. And he had a hard job holding down shortstop's berth. He was light and rather frail looking. But for all that, he played in more consecutive ball-games than any other ballplayer. He never seemed to get hurt.

"Ty Cobb played at top speed longer than anybody else. He never spared himself, always went ahead with every ounce of steam. And he never seemed to get hurt. He was no rugged stevedore. No doubt he had a good deal of strength, but it was rangy strength rather than bulgy. It wasn't strength that kept him going either. Durable players last a long while, not so much because they are stronger than other players, but because they are wiry and have the knack of avoiding injuries.

"On the contrary, some players are brittle. They always seem to be bunged up, on the shelf for repairs. A certain amount of this may be hard luck, but it's pretty likely to be something else. They can't stand the pace.

"In my case, I suppose, it's just beef and natural dumbness. At least that's what my old buddy used to say. 'You're as big as a truck horse and you ought to be able to stand more mauling than two ordinary players.' Perhaps he was right.

"I'm big enough, I guess." Here he stretched himself to his full height. "And I suppose size is an advantage to a pitcher. In fact, I know it is. When I reach forward to deliver the ball, I'm nearer the plate than a lot of other pitchers. I suppose I can lop off a foot or so from the average pitching distance. That's an item.

"Besides, throwing the ball on a slant downward, you can count on the attraction of gravitation to help you out. They build up the pitching mounds to help the medium-sized pitcher. If you're six or eight inches taller than the average player, the same as I am, you have that additional advantage.

"I suppose it's a repetition of the boxing formula, 'A good big man is better than a good little man.' Most managers like good-sized pitchers. They think they can stand the work better, and there's something in that theory.

"No doubt my height and reach and weight have a good deal to do with my pitching fair ball at this stage of the game. But I think that the wear and tear of big-league games is mental quite as much as physical. Every ballplayer broods more or less, in spite of what some of them tell you. When a pitcher has lost five or six straight games, there's no sense in expecting him to feel cheerful. When a batter's in a slump, it's the same thing. I worry as little as most people, but I know how depressing it is when you've lost two or three ballgames in a row.

"The worst game to lose is the one that you count already in. A slip or two in the ninth inning and it got away from you. It's easy to look back on a lost game and figure how it might have been saved. I've known pitchers who did so much of that thing, they couldn't sleep nights.

"Bill Carrigan uttered a mouthful of wisdom when he said, 'If your job worries you, give up your job.' Sheer worry has shortened the careers of more ballplayers than any other one cause.

"Batters figure there are two kinds of slumps. One is due to luck, one to poor hitting. Pitchers figure the same way. A game may be lost because of poor work on the slab. It may be lost in spite of good work on the slab. Both of them count for the same zero in the percentage column, but they don't leave the same impression on the pitcher. He knows when he's done good work as well as anyone else.

"No doubt the pitcher ought to feel worse about games that he has lost because of his own poor work. But a lot of them seem to be more cut up about the other kind. It's easier to excuse yourself than the other fellow. If you've lost through your own poor work, you can feel you had a beating coming to you. But when you've really pitched a good game and lost through errors or some other way not your fault, you're inclined to feel that you've been robbed.

"There's a certain amount of excuse for this. A pitcher's work, more than that of other ballplayers, stands or falls with that of his own club. A batter can hit .400 on a tail-end team and be considered a great batter. A pitcher, unless he's a superman, can't drag a whole ballclub very far up the grade by his own exertions. When he's pitched good enough ball to win and hasn't won, he's likely to feel peeved. I know, for I've had plenty of experience.

"There's one favor you might do me," said Rixey, reverting to his characteristic semiserious, semicomic attitude. "You know that

'Jeptha' thing they keep tacking on to my name. That's excess baggage. I didn't get a very good deal anyway, in names. But Jeptha is rubbing it in, and it's not true. Eppa is authentic. I plead guilty and throw myself on the mercy of the court. But Jeptha I deny. Don't you think Eppa is enough?" And he gave me a look of sad resignation such as could come only from long years of patient suffering.

Eppa *is* enough. Eppa Rixey suffices for all six feet and six inches of him; quaint, humorous, and genial, one of the greatest southpaws who ever donned a mitt or toed a hurling slab.

Stanley Frank, *The Cincinnati Post*

VANDER MEER ON PINNACLE

Pitching consecutive no-hitters seems an unimaginable feat, and it's one that's been done just once in the history of major league baseball. Johnny Vander Meer tossed the back-to-back gems for the Reds in 1938, shutting down the Boston Bees on June 11, and then the Dodgers on June 15 in the first-ever night game played at Brooklyn's Ebbets Field. The Cincinnati Post's Stanley Frank covered the second no-hitter in Brooklyn and authored the following article.

Miracles do happen. Events beyond all credulity are yet to be seen. Johnny Vander Meer, 23-year-old Cincinnati southpaw, has pitched two successive no-hit, no-run ballgames, an achievement without parallel and never to be exceeded until there is improvement upon perfection.

In the 99-year history of baseball there have been 115 no-hit, no-run games pitched by 105 men in the major leagues. L.J. Corcoran pitched three no-hitters for the Cubs in the 1880s. Seven other men—including Christy Mathewson, Cy Young, and Hub Leonard—pitched two.

But until Vander Meer duplicated his feat of last Saturday, when he held the Bees hitless and scoreless, by defeating the Dodgers, 6–0, at Ebbets Field last night before a mob of 38,740 hysterical psychopaths, technically known as baseball fans watching the first night game in Brooklyn, no man had ever pitched no-hitters in two successive appearances on the mound.

For five agonizing minutes in the ninth inning it seemed that the kid might get his no-hitter but not his no-runner. With one out Vander Meer, working under terrific tension, lost his control, and walked three straight Dodgers to fill the bases. A fly ball to the outfield, a deep grounder to the infield, would score the run that would make the brilliant performance as flat as an uncorked bottle of champagne. The roaring, capacity mob was pulling frantically for the boy, who was practically unknown a month ago and today is the most prominent sports celebrity in the broad land. Loyalty to the home team was forgotten. The fans knew Vander Meer was on the threshold of that which passes for immortality in baseball and they wanted him to get it. Wanted it desperately, as much as Vander Meer, who still had a ball-game to win and a no-hit, no-run game to hope for with all the power and deception in his flailing left arm.

Ernie Koy, who hit a home run off Vander Meer two weeks ago, was the next Dodgers batter. A tremendously fast man—a few hours previously he had defeated Jesse Owens, Olympic sprint champion, with the aid of a 10-yard handicap in an exhibition race—Koy offered little possibility of a double play, which would end the game. Vander Meer was strictly on his own. And he was tired.

Riggs Plays It Safe

He shot across a fast strike, then Koy ticked one foul. There was a called ball. And then there was the sight and sound of Koy's bat making contact with the ball. It went directly to Lew Riggs, the third baseman, on two big hops. Koy got a late start from the plate; Riggs could still gamble for a double play by way of second.

But he played it the safe way. Vander Meer's way. Riggs carefully sighted and threw to Ernie Lombardi at the plate, forcing pinch runner Goody Rosen. Two out; one to go for the most astonishing feat baseball has seen since Abner Doubleday came up with a bright idea at Cooperstown, New York, in 1839.

Leo Durocher was the last man between Vander Meer and his no-hitter. Any major leaguer with a bat in his hands is dangerous; any number of no-hitters have been ruined with two out in the ninth. The mob howled for Durocher to strike out, make out any way he pleased. But make out. Durocher, a tough, hard-boiled citizen, dug in at the plate. A strike was called, then a ball. Durocher swung hard at the next pitch and missed. He fouled one into the grandstand. And then he sent a high, soft fly out to center field.

Knew He Had No-Hitter

It looked like a "blooper," a lucky Texas Leaguer for a moment. The mob held its breath, then exploded with a roar of relief when Harry Craft, the Reds' center fielder, charged in 10 yards, waved his colleagues away, and camped under the descending ball.

As soon as it had settled in his glove there was a race between the fans and Vander Meer. The kid was racing for the safety of the dugout. The fans were racing to pat him on the back, perhaps to tear the shirt off his back as a souvenir of a historic night. A few fans intercepted him, but they were brushed aside by his teammates, who rushed him through the crowd.

"This time I knew I was working on a no-hitter," Vander Meer said in the clubhouse when Bill McKechnie, his manager, finally permitted him to be interviewed. "Last Saturday, against the Bees, I didn't know I hadn't given a hit until it was all over.

"I really didn't begin to think I had a chance to pitch two in a row until the seventh inning, though. Nobody on the bench said a word to me. Didn't want to put the whammy on me, I guess. How many did I walk? Eight? That's because I was bearing down so hard to go through. It's pretty hard to believe yet that I did. No, I don't think the lights helped me very much. I had pretty good stuff tonight."

For once a ballplayer was not guilty of overstatement. Durocher, captain of the Dodgers and a veteran of 11 seasons in the big leagues, more or less summed up the attitude of his team.

"Vander Meer had more speed and stuff tonight than I've ever seen in baseball," Durocher said.

There was nothing fishy about Vander Meer's epic accomplishment. Neither the base umpires nor the official scorer had a difficult decision to make. The closest approach to a Brooklyn hit came in the first inning when Buddy Hassett drove a sharp grounder back to the box. Vander Meer deflected the ball with his glove and slowed it up just enough to permit Lonny Frey, his second baseman, to make a good recovery and throw to first to nip Hassett, a fast man.

Otherwise, the Dodgers went up and presently went down. Vander Meer fanned seven, handled six fielding chances himself, and allowed only four balls to be hit to the outfield.

Vander Meer's mother, father, and best girl were given a brisk workout by reporters and photographers until their hero emerged from the clubhouse. They were, of course, beaming all over the place. So were 500 rooters from Midland Park, New Jersey, John's hometown, who traveled to Ebbets Field by bus to present him with a gold watch before the game. An hour after it was all over there were hundreds of fans waiting for the Great Man's autograph.

Brooklyn had him at training camp in 1933 but he drifted away. The Bees had him and let him go. Strangely enough, the two clubs that might own Vander Meer today were the victims of his blazing fastball and his sharp curve.

One Hit in 26 Innings

Among other things, Vander Meer now has a stretch of pitching that threatens every record in the books. In his last 26 innings he has given exactly one hit. On June 5 the Giants got to him for two hits in the first inning, then made one more thereafter, a dinky single to center by Hank Leiber. He followed up with his no-hitter against the Bees on Saturday and last night again was invincible.

His record for the season shows seven victories against two defeats and six of those winning decisions have come successively. During that stretch he has given three runs and 18 hits. Matty, Young, Bender,

Walsh, Plank, Johnson, Alexander, Grove, Dean, Hubbell—any number of pitchers may be recognized as better pitchers than Vander Meer when he has completed his career, but no man who ever lived is hotter than the Fogging Dutchman right now.

The customers went to Ebbets Field last night for their first view of night baseball out of curiosity. They went away with the biggest thrill of their lives. It was a rare privilege to see Vander Meer, a boy, doing a man's job on history. And they knew it.

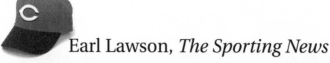

Earl Lawson, *The Sporting News*

NUXHALL EYES LONG RED RUN WITH SLIP PITCH AND SINKER

Just 15 years, 10 months, and 11 days old when he made his major league debut with the Reds on June 10, 1944, Joe Nuxhall had a disastrous outing, giving up five runs in just two-thirds of an inning. It took him seven years to return to the majors after that initial appearance, and he made the most of it. Nuxhall pitched all but one season of his career with the Reds before retiring just before Opening Day in 1967 to take a place in the Reds' broadcast booth. He was a wily veteran at the time Earl Lawson wrote the following piece for The Sporting News *in 1963.*

It wasn't so long ago that Joe Nuxhall was punching holes through backstop screens with his errant fastballs. The catcher needed a fish net, the hitter life insurance.

Today, the 34-year-old left-hander is classified as a control artist. And he finds this almost as unbelievable as the circuitous route he traveled last year that led him back to the Reds where he compiled an equally fascinating 5–0 record after his purchase from San Diego in midseason.

"Yep, a year can make quite a difference," agreed Nuxhall, who this time last year appeared to be reaching the end of a career that began when he was still a fuzzy-cheeked 15-year-old schoolboy.

Nuxhall, after having received his unconditional release from the Athletics, had caught on with the Rochester (International) club. Baltimore, which had a working agreement with Rochester, had promised him a chance to make the Orioles in spring training.

But a guy can't live on promises because, as Joe puts it, "I like to eat too well."

Baltimore gave Nuxhall his walking papers.

Short Stint in Baltimore

"We think you can still pitch in the majors, but we want to go with youngsters," Orioles manager Billy Hitchcock told him last spring.

He later caught on with the Angels, and all they told him a few weeks later when he got the pink slip was, "Good-bye."

Nuxhall thinks the Angels made a mistake bouncing him before he had a chance to pitch. Today, the Angels probably agree.

Nuxhall, signing with the Reds' San Diego (Coast) club, won nine and lost two to earn a promotion to the Reds.

With the Reds, his perfect record was accompanied by a gaudy 2.45 earned-run mark.

You can't say he was lucky because the way his luck has run in the past, he'd have a hard time winning at craps with loaded dice.

"Anything can happen at my age," said Nuxhall. "It's a funny stage of a pitcher's career. Look at Warren Spahn. He has had some of his greatest seasons since he was 34."

Nuxhall chuckled. "I'm not a Spahn maybe," he said, "but who knows, if I perfect my slip pitch and get a little better sinkerball, I could be pitching in the majors for seven or eight more years."

He didn't sound as if he were a guy who was worried about the arm trouble that sidelined him during the final weeks of the 1962 season.

"That was just a strained tendon in my elbow," he said, shrugging off the injury. "I got it by favoring my leg after I pulled a muscle in that game in Chicago. There's no tenderness now and I've been playing handball and lifting weights all winter. The last few days I've even been throwing a little in the YMCA here at Hamilton."

Nuxhall reported that he has shed 15 pounds since the end of the season.

"I'm down to 223 pounds," he said. "Of course, I ballooned up pretty good at the end of the season when I couldn't run or pitch."

Operates Service Station

Joe also has gone into the filling station business at Fairfield, just outside of Hamilton, Ohio, which is some 20 miles from Cincinnati.

"I think a lot of people are staying away because they think I don't know anything about cars. And they're right. I don't," the vet hurler said, laughing.

"But I can put gas in a tank and pour oil in a car and we've got a mechanic here who can do any work that's required on a car."

Nuxhall hastened to explain, though, that he's not preparing for his retirement.

"Like I said," he repeated, "I think I've got a few good years left in my pitching arm."

The veteran lefty credits the slip pitch as being responsible for much of his success last year.

"Harry Brecheen showed me how to throw it last spring when I was training with Baltimore," he said.

Nuxhall used the pitch sparingly when he was with San Diego. "I used it a lot more after I joined the Reds," he explained.

For this, Hank Foiles, the Reds catcher, was responsible.

"Hank was with me when I trained with Baltimore," explained Nuxhall. "I had lost the knack of throwing the slip pitch at San Diego. When I joined the Reds, I worked it out with Hank. And it was darn effective."

Nuxhall claims that "improved control" was another reason for his success with the Reds last year.

"Heck," he said, grinning, "I got so I could even hit spots."

And that is quite an achievement for a guy who once handed out more free tickets than a press agent.

"I have some reasons for the improved control," said Nuxhall.

"One," he said, "is I'm not working as fast as I used to. I'm thinking ahead all the time, trying to set up the batter for a certain pitch. And if I miss on a pitch, I'm not getting mad at myself. That's what I used to do and I'd always wind up trying to fog the ball past a hitter."

Arthur Daley, *The New York Times*

WITH HIBERNIAN OVERTONES

One of key performers on the Reds' surprising 1961 pennant winner, lefty Jim O'Toole combined with right-handers Joey Jay and Bob Purkey to give Cincinnati the solid pitching punch the team had lacked in previous years. O'Toole won 19 games with a 3.10 ERA in '61 and also started twice in the World Series against the Yankees. He continued to have success the next three seasons, posting records of 16–13, 17–14, and 17–7. Winning just three times in 1965, O'Toole was traded to the White Sox and his pitching days ended with a shoulder injury in 1967. Arthur Daley's article on O'Toole appeared in the March 22, 1962, edition of The New York Times.

Jimmy O'Toole of the Reds rounded third base on his way to score in a game last season when he inexplicably fell. He scrambled back toward third in embarrassment and was even more embarrassed to discover that burly Eddie Mathews of the Braves was waiting for him with the ball. O'Toole, a forthright young man, attempted to jostle the ball from Mathews's hand. The 200-pound Mathews came up swinging.

At the first sign of a fight a powerfully built man in a front box swung his leg over the rail to start toward the scuffle. He was Bill O'Toole, a Chicago police captain and the father of the Cincinnati pitcher. But another son yanked him back into the box.

"Jimmy's a big boy now, Pop," said the son. "He doesn't need help. He can take care of himself."

He sure can. The 200-pound pride of the O'Tooles swiftly clamped a headlock on the pugnacious Mathews and rode him to the ground like a cowpuncher bulldogging a steer. Then Jimmy sat on him until he calmed down.

Mass Strangulation

The Milwaukee slugger wasn't the only hitter the 25-year-old left-hander throttled last season. The cocky kid with the whistling fast ball, the dimpled chin, and the taunting hazel eyes was a 19-game winner for the National League champions. He's as good as he thinks he is—which is plenty—and figures to be a top-grade pitcher for a long time to come, even though he didn't have it today against the Orioles.

Cincinnati snatched O'Toole away from Detroit in December of 1957 by making adroit use of its Irish Mafia. This slick group of Blarney Stone–kissers had Paul Florence as its chief agent in the field, assisted by his brother-in-law, Bill Sullivan. At headquarters was Birdie Tebbetts, then the Reds' manager.

Detroit was outnumbered, having only George Moriarty, a former umpire and manager. But Moriarty had discovered James Jerome O'Toole as a precocious 14-year-old in Chicago when the boy fanned all 21 hitters he faced in a seven-inning sandlot game. The Tiger scout also was close to O'Toole Sr., whose ancestors didn't come from Outer Slobovia.

Added Weight

It was Florence who arranged for a Redleg tryout. It was viewed in goggle-eyed wonder by Tebbetts and by his first assistant, Jimmie Dykes, whose forebears also played the harp that once through Tara's Halls, etc.

"If I were your father," said Birdie to the boy, using the paternal technique, "and if I had a son who wanted to be a big-leaguer, I'd be most interested in a team like ours. We have the best defense and the best power in the league. We have everything but pitching and that's why you can advance faster with us than anyone else." He grinned and added, "Besides, there are not too many of us Irish left."

Just in case that Celtic appeal was not sufficient of itself, the Reds also offered a $50,000 bonus. Jimmy was touched. But he couldn't follow the leanings of his heart, mind, and pocketbook until he'd kept his promise of first refusal to Moriarty. So he told the Tiger scout that he had decided against returning to the University of Wisconsin for his final two years and would take the Cincinnati offer unless....

"But you're not ready," said Moriarty, starting to spout sparks.

"Can you do better?" asked Jimmy. Moriarty, who was not ready either, began to explode.

"You're an ingrate," fumed Moriarty. "You're just a shanty Irishman."

Because this is a phrase that only an Irishman is privileged to use against another, O'Toole laughed at him and signed with the Reds. In less than a season at Nashville in 1958, he was ready.

Wrong Pairing

But Jimmy laughs easily even though he's a bear-down competitor. One day last season he foozled three bunts in a row, and Freddie Hutchinson, his manger, came stampeding to the mound in a black rage.

"What goes on here?" roared Hutch, fierce and formidable.

"I gave it my best shot, Babe," said the flippant Jimmy.

"Listen, Babe," retorted Hutch, stifling a smile, "it looks as though your best isn't good enough." Then Hutch had to flee before laughter routed discipline.

It was O'Toole, bold and unafraid, who drew the pressure-filled job of pitching the opening game of the World Series. He lost it, and the fourth game, too.

"I just happened to draw Whitey Ford both times when he was breaking Babe Ruth's record for scoreless innings," he now can say with a carefree shrug.

"I'll tell you what was my best and biggest game of last year," he continued. "We were in a do-or-die series with Los Angeles. Joey Jay won the first game, 5–3, or some such score. Then came a double-header. Bob Purkey pitched a 6–0 shutout for us, and I hammered the last nail in the coffin by pitching an 8–0 shutout, a two-hitter."

It's no wonder that Moriarty blew his top when he lost O'Toole to the Reds. This jaunty Irishman is a rare prize.

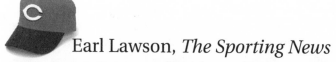

Earl Lawson, *The Sporting News*

NL HURLERS' CREDO— DON'T RILE ROBBY

Slugger Frank Robinson terrorized National League pitchers for 10 seasons in Cincinnati, winning the 1961 NL MVP award as he led the Reds to their first pennant in 21 years. A six-time All-Star for Cincinnati, Robinson was traded to the Baltimore Orioles with prospect Dick Simpson for pitchers Milt Pappas and Jack Baldschun. The deal, in all fairness, is the worst in Reds' history. Robinson was enjoying another stellar season in 1965 when Earl Lawson authored this article for the May 22, 1965, issue of The Sporting News.

Average-wise, Frankie Robinson may not be the best hitter in baseball, but there's none more aggressive at the plate.

"You see Roberto Clemente get a lot of hits with his backside in the dugout," Don Zimmer, the ex-National Leaguer once observed. "And there are times when Willie Mays and Hank Aaron bail out a little while they're winging, but Robby never. He's always stepping into a pitch."

The 29-year-old Reds slugger, who stands in the batter's box with his left elbow protruding almost halfway across the plate, offers an inviting target to pitchers.

But those pitchers who have deliberately thrown at him in an effort to push him away from the plate generally have wound up regretting it. Robinson won't be intimidated.

"I've found that the best way to retaliate is with a base hit," says Robby. "There's no sense in getting into a fight. You might wind up with an injury. Then you're out of the lineup. You just hurt your own team."

Robby's mode of retaliation is so effective that Gene Mauch, the Phillie manager, has established an automatic fine for any pitcher on his club who deliberately throws at the Reds slugger.

Mauch Makes Sense

"Robinson is trouble enough any time. Get him riled and you've just got more trouble," is the way Mauch puts it.

The Dodgers learned this the hard way.

It was July 9, 1961. In the first inning, Robby homered off Roger Craig, now one of his teammates. He drew a walk in the second and then singled off Sandy Koufax in the fifth inning. In the sixth inning, Don Drysdale drew an automatic fine after plunking Robby.

With Dick Farrell pitching for the Dodgers in the eighth inning, Robby retaliated with his second homer of the game. He socked a bases-loaded double in the ninth inning.

The Reds wound up winning, 14–3.

Robinson's contribution included two homers, a single and double, and seven RBIs. He also walked and was hit by a pitch.

There are many other examples, like last year at San Francisco. Robby, after being hit by a pitched ball, got into a rhubarb with the Giants. During the yakking that took place, Robby and Gaylord Perry, the Giants hurler, exchanged heated words.

The next day, Perry started against the Reds. Robby tagged him for a home run the first time he went to the plate.

Felled by Pascual Pitch

Even though he perennially leads the league in getting hit by pitched balls, Robby has been seriously injured only once in his career.

This was in the spring of 1958 during an exhibition game in Portsmouth, Ohio, when fastballer Camillo Pascual of the Twins hit the Reds slugger on the left temple just below his protective helmet.

Robby dropped to the ground as if felled by a bullet and was carried off to the hospital.

"That won't bother him. He has been hit in the head before," Birdie Tebbetts, then the Reds manager, remarked as Robby lay on a table in the hospital's receiving room.

It was true; Robby had been hit in the head before by pitches. On the other occasions, though, the protective helmet had absorbed most of the blow.

As Robby lay on the table, he wondered to himself how long his luck was going to last. Would the next time be worse?

During the first half of the 1958 season, Robinson admitted he fought plate shyness. At the All-Star break, he was batting under .250, had hit only eight homers, and had driven home only 23 runs.

23 Homers in 80 Games

However, in the Reds' final 80 games of the 1958 season, Robby socked 23 homers and drove home 60 runs.

"At the beginning of the season," he later explained, "I kept telling myself I wasn't afraid. Still, I couldn't keep from rolling back on my heels every time a pitcher curved me. Then all of a sudden I wasn't falling back anymore. I guess I got so mad at myself I didn't care what happened."

Robinson wound up with a .269 mark for the 1958 season. Only once has he hit for a lower average. This was in 1963, when he skidded to .259.

During that 1963 season, Robby was plagued by one nagging injury after another. Then, too, he was forced to make adjustments at the plate when opposing pitchers began serving up a steady stream of off-speed pitches.

"In the past," pointed out the Reds slugger, "pitchers had always tried to jam me with fastballs inside because I stand so close to the plate."

Last year, Robby bounced back with a .306 batting average, tops on the club. Still, he was far from satisfied.

"I get paid to hit homers and drive home runs," said Robby, who ranks as the highest-paid player in Reds history.

100 RBIs Robby's Minimum

"And," he added, "any time I don't hit 30 or more homers and drive home 100 or more runs, I feel I haven't had a real good year."

This is Robinson's 10th year with the Reds.

Only three times has he failed to hit 30 or more homers.

As a 20-year-old rookie back in 1956, Robby batted .290, socked 38 homers and drove home 83 runs to win unanimous acclaim as the league's Rookie of the Year.

His 38 homers topped a fence-busting array of Reds sluggers who walloped a total of 221 home runs to tie a major league record.

Five years later—1961—Robby batted .323, socked 37 homers, and drove home 124 runs to lead the Reds to their first pennant in 21 years.

Baseball writers voted him the league's Most Valuable Player.

Robby experienced an even better season in 1962, batting a rousing .342 while almost single-handedly carrying the Reds to a second straight high finish.

His 134 runs scored in 1962 led the league. So did his 51 doubles. He hit 39 homers and drove home 136 runs, both career highs.

The fact that Wally Post still holds the club record for most homers by a right-handed batter (40) irks Robby.

"I've hit 39, 38, 37, and 36," he pointed out, "so I know I can hit 40 or more."

He's hoping this will be the year.

Post's club record is one of the few that have eluded Robby during his career with the Reds.

He already owns the all-time club records for runs scored, doubles, home runs, total bases, extra-base hits, and slugging percentage.

Lifetime Bat Mark .304

After nine years with the Reds, he owns a lifetime batting mark of .304. He'll join the National League's exclusive 300-homer club this season and, if he drives home 104 or more runs, he'll reach the 1,000 mark in career RBIs.

Actually, Robby's looking forward to one of the most productive seasons of his career.

Batting ahead of him this season are Pete Rose, Tommy Harper, and Vada Pinson.

"Among them, they should be on base about 700 times," figures Robby. "If I'm right, I'll consider it a poor year if I don't drive home more than 100 runs."

The switch of Deron Johnson to third to make room for sluggers Tony Perez and Gordy Coleman at first figures to benefit Robby, too.

"Pitchers," pointed out Reds manager Dick Sisler, "will be less likely to try to pitch around Robby."

It was Robinson's strong wrists that impressed Tebbetts most when Frankie joined the Reds as a rookie 10 years ago.

"The guy can hold up a swing right in the middle of the plate," Tebbetts had exclaimed. "Ted Williams is one of the few other hitters I've seen who can do that."

"He's so quick with his wrists," Jimmie Dykes, then an aid to Tebbetts, remarked, "he can literally hit a ball out of a catcher's glove." Robby, like most of the game's superstars, can beat a club three ways—with his bat, his arm, and his glove.

Great Instinct on Bases

There are a number of players in the majors who surpass Robinson in speed, but few have his base-running instincts.

"Robby knows how to get a good jump on a pitcher," the late Fred Hutchinson once said. "And when he goes for an extra base, you can almost bet he'll make it."

In each of the last four seasons, Robby stole 18 or more bases.

As a competitor, Robby is one of the most fierce the game has known. For example, there was the doubleheader with the Braves during the 1960 season.

In the first game, Eddie Mathews, the Braves' third baseman, thought Robby slid into him too hard and said so. One word led to another and, in a matter of seconds, Robby and Mathews were exchanging swings.

Robby, catching a hard right flush on the right eye, went to the ground with Mathews on top of him. When the fight was broken up, Robby went to the clubhouse for repairs. He insisted upon playing the second game, even though his right eye was practically swollen shut.

The Reds went on to win the game with Robinson contributing a double and a two-run homer. He also robbed Mathews of an extra-base hit by snaring a liner off the Braves third baseman's bat while diving headlong into the left-field stands.

"That's the best way to get even," an admiring Mathews later commented.

"The guy has absolutely no fear of fences," said Sisler.

There are a lot of players in the majors, perhaps, who boast stronger arms than Robinson, but few are more accurate.

Speedy Lou Brock of the Cardinals learned this the hard way on April 24.

Brock was nailed at the plate by a Robinson strike as he attempted to score from second on Dick Groat's single.

Robinson was first spotted by former Reds scout Bobby Mattick as a skinny 14-year-old playing American Legion Junior baseball in Oakland, California.

Oddly enough, Mattick had attended the game to scout another outfielder, J.W. Porter, who later was signed for a handsome bonus by the White Sox. Porter, incidentally, bounced around the American League a few years and then dropped into oblivion.

Robinson was an immediate success in organized ball, batting .348 and slamming 17 homers for the Reds' Ogden club in the old Pioneer League after signing a pro contract in June of 1953.

Hurt Arm in Puerto Rico

The next year, he batted .336 and socked 25 homers for the Reds' Columbia farm club of the old Sally League. And, if he hadn't contracted an arm ailment playing winter ball in Puerto Rico after the 1954 season, he might have joined the Cincinnati club in 1955 instead of a year later.

Because of the arm ailment, Robby played first base for Columbia in 1955.

"I couldn't throw from first base to the pitcher's mound without wincing in pain," he recalled. "The arm sometimes became so swollen I couldn't put on a jacket."

Late in 1955, though, the soreness in Robby's arm disappeared as mysteriously as it came. No longer handicapped, he began socking the ball with his old-time vigor and finished the 1955 season with a .263 mark and 12 homers in 243 trips to the plate.

"If Robinson can throw from the outfield to second base, he's my left fielder," Tebbetts remarked in the spring of 1956.

Robby not only was the Reds' left fielder, but he wound up occupying the same position for the National League in the 1956 All-Star Game.

He has been an All-Star ever since.

George Vecsey, *Sport* magazine

JOHNNY BENCH, THE MAN BEHIND THE MASK

The greatest catcher of all time? Quite possibly. His list of accomplish-
ments and awards is long and impressive: 10 Gold Gloves, two MVP
awards, 12 All-Star Games, and 389 career home runs. Still, it was behind
the plate where Bench really excelled, and invariably his defensive skill
set would turn games around more often than his slugging. "I can throw
out any man alive," he once said—and he could. After a down year, by
Bench standards, in 1971, George Vecsey authored the following piece for
Sport magazine about Bench's, and the Reds', resurgence in 1972.

One steamy weekend this July, I was in Cincinnati to do a story about
Johnny Bench. I had quit covering baseball about the time Johnny
Bench became a superstar, so I had never met the man. Everybody
knows about the Most Valuable Player award at 22, the 114 homers by
his 24th birthday, the autographed baseball from Ted Williams that said:
"To Johnny Bench—a Hall of Famer for sure." Now I was going back
into baseball for a steamy weekend in Cincinnati to find out what kind
of a man Johnny Bench really is, coming off a year of trouble in 1971,
but back on top again in 1972.

There are times when it seems somebody has jabbed a dose of
truth serum into Sparky Anderson's arm. He gets into these talking
jags, with all these fine, personal theories in his head, and they've just
got to come out. Sparky Anderson is from South Dakota. People from
South Dakota always tell the truth.

"To me, John stands for a lot of good things about the young
people in America," Sparky Anderson said early on that Friday
evening, watching his players amble into the clubhouse. "John thinks
about things. He separates his ideas carefully. The young people are
against all that killing over there. Somebody my age [Sparky is all of 38]
might not be so much against that killing—but the young people are.
Maybe they'll stop us from killing each other. Somebody's got to. I've
talked to John about things like that. I know how he feels. He's for
young people 'doing their thing.' He's a good person."

The manager of the Reds sometimes wonders if other people object to his open admiration for his young catcher. He admits that people call him and Bench "bobo's." It means they're close.

"John's got class," Sparky continued. "Baseball needs men like him. Baseball's got to keep people like John in the game. I think it's great that Ted Williams came back as a manager. The superstars should be kept around as managers—if they can handle men. Williams can communicate. Bench can, too. I think John's got the ability to manage—if he wants to."

Bench was standing by the batting cage. It was a typical hectic night for him. Club officials were calling him in three directions at once to shake hands with important guests. His grandmother was flying in for the game. The Reds were fighting to hold on to first place. His picture had just been on the cover of *Time* magazine. He had Army Reserve duty at dawn on Sunday, smack in the middle of four games in 48 hours. It seemed likely that any further publicity at this point would be meaningless to him. It was really a matter of whether he felt like being interviewed.

He looked me up and down with a purposeful, intelligent scrutiny, out of strong gray eyes. People have described him as a young man who would have become a bank executive if he hadn't become a catcher. He struck me more as a commander of a state trooper post, the guy who makes decisions and deals with the public, not just a guy who gives out tickets. Or maybe a young officer in the Civil War (either side), dedicated to his duty but not exactly giddy over war. Authoritative. Like, if he strolled out to the mound and said, "Bust your butt," a pitcher would bust his butt.

"You'll be around for a few days," he said flatly. "We'll talk."

Al Michaels is a slick young announcer who believes announcers can be reporters, too. He keeps his eyes open in the booth while broadcasting the Reds' games.

"You get used to Bench doing something fantastic," Michaels said, sitting in the dugout, watching batting practice. "When he doesn't come through, you feel kind of let down. I know that's ridiculous, since all players make outs most of the time. But when Bench makes an out, you're almost...disillusioned. Does that make sense?

"Even on defense, you're surprised when a ball gets through him. I think everybody is. We played a game in New York when a pitch went right through him. I think I know a passed ball when I see one. I couldn't believe it—but that's how I described it. After the game, the official scorer went down to the clubhouse to check what had happened. He found out the pitcher had crossed Bench up on the signal. So he gave the pitcher a wild pitch.

"Can you imagine an official scorer checking a passed ball for any catcher but Bench? I guess the scorer didn't believe it, either."

A legend at 24. A legend to the men who work with him. A legend to the people in the stands. The license plates in the Cincinnati parking lot indicate that fathers have driven across the river from Kentucky, from the hidden coal villages of West Virginia, driven all morning across the flatlands of Indiana, barreled up at dawn from Knoxville. And the fathers are probably telling the sons: "That's Johnny Bench. Take a good look at him. He's got to be one of the greatest players that ever lived."

That's what fathers told their sons in New York 20 years ago, about another kid from Oklahoma. But even a child could tell there was something desperate about young Mickey Mantle, the way he tore the batting helmet from his head, the way the fans booed him when he struck out, the way his neck and face flushed red.

Later the fans turned toward Mantle because of his magnificent courage and performances. But it was too late for him to really enjoy it. He once confessed to me, in one of our rare conversations, that he didn't understand what fans in Boston and New York were talking about.

What a terrible burden, to make a living in some foreign town, to play before strangers. There was a story this spring that Bench had decided not to tip his cap to Cincinnati fans this year because they booed him in 1971. Was it the Mantle thing all over again, the deep distrust of the crowd?

If it could happen to the kid from Commerce, couldn't it also happen to the kid from Binger (population: 730, "Two miles past the 'Resume Speed' sign," Bench once described his home)?

It had all happened so fast. Like Mantle, Bench was prepared to be a baseball player by a father who had wanted to be a major leaguer himself. Ted Bench organized a Little League team once, just so John could play, and later he drove John 17 miles to another league.

In the high school years, John won 16 out of 17 pitching decisions (he believes he could "get 'em out" in the majors today), batting .675 at the same time. He was signed by the Reds in 1965 and roared through the minor leagues in less than three seasons. They retired his number at Peninsula for hitting 22 homers. He hit 23 homers at Buffalo in 1967, but the only number they gave him was the flight number to Cincinnati. That was fine.

The next year he was an All-Star catcher at the age of 20. Then he was Most Valuable Player at 22, then slumping at 23, then threatening not to tip his cap at 24. Could the gentle folk in baseball's smallest major league city turn him sour, the way the biggest city drove Mantle into a shell?

"Cincinnati is different from New York," Sparky Anderson said. "They don't give you that much publicity here. Geez, when the Mets won the World Series, even Rod Gaspar was a big man."

The big man wore No. 5 on this muggy Saturday in Riverfront Stadium, one of those new and anonymous stadiums that were seemingly designed to steam human beings like shrimp on hot afternoons.

Bench drove in a run in the first inning, slapping a two-out single. Then the Reds and the Cubs struggled to the bottom of the seventh, locked at 2–2. But Gary Nolan led off with a single, Joe Morgan flied out, Pete Rose walked, and Bobby Tolan forced Rose at second. That brought up Bench with two outs.

The fathers nudged their sons; the sons screamed with anticipation; even characterless Riverfront Stadium almost came alive. This was the moment the fans had driven downtown to see: Johnny Bench in the clutch.

Leo Durocher, as usual, had waited too long to lift his starting pitcher, a kid named Rick Reuschel. (It was the kind of nonaction that would finally get Leo fired on July 25.) Leo did get around to bringing in Dan McGinn to face Tolan. Then he called for Tom Phoebus to face Bench. Phoebus, a stubby little right-hander with a seemingly outsized head, trudged in from the bullpen, his steps seeming to grow slower and shorter as he neared the mound. If ever a pitcher looked like a victim, Phoebus did.

Bench helped heighten the impression when he approached the batting box. He flexed his shoulders, turned his head sideways, fixed his high-cheekboned stare at Phoebus. It was the kind of moment Al Michaels had described, where you almost expected Bench to come through. Yet the statistics showed that Bench was only a career .271 hitter. Was this one of those 271 times out of a thousand?

Phoebus caught the outside corner of the plate and Bench took it for a strike. The fans grew louder. Then Bench got way ahead of an outside pitch and tipped it away. Two strikes. Last year Bench was often clumsy and overeager with two strikes, not sure whether to try for a homer or protect the plate, often accomplishing neither.

This time he took a level swing, slashing a line drive to center field. Nolan scored easily from third base as the fans screamed more. Everybody sensed it would be the last run of the game. With Tommy Hall pitching in relief, it was. The fans waded happily through the postgame traffic jam. Johnny Bench hadn't let them down.

"You're still here," Johnny Bench said carefully. "You're quiet—but you hang in there."

It was after the Saturday game and Bench was relaxing in the clubhouse, concentrating on a Bobby Fischer chess special on television. He had driven in two runs in a 3–2 victory. He talked about a number of things and then I brought up the Mantle/New York syndrome.

"I know Mickey," Bench said in a measured way. "I've played golf with him a few times but we've never talked that much about baseball. Mickey's usually got his own friends around him. But I can understand the New York scene. Coming from Oklahoma, I can see where you learn that people have their come-ons. Everybody says they're going to do you a favor. After a while, you become leery and guarded."

I mentioned how I thought of Mantle when I saw the movie *The Last Picture Show,* a poignant look at growing up in a raw Texas town. Then try transplanting a country boy into the major leagues....

"I really appreciated that picture," Bench said, his face showing enthusiasm for the first time. "I went to that picture here in Cincinnati and at times I was the only one laughing. The people from the city couldn't appreciate some of the things in the movie."

He stared at the moody genius of Bobby Fischer on the television screen, one champion evaluating another. Then he turned sideways again.

"Growing up in Oklahoma, Mickey Mantle was my idol," he said. "But when I heard about Lou Boudreau managing the Cleveland Indians at the age of 24, Boudreau became my idol. I'd like to be considered for managing some day," he continued. "I talk to Sparky on the bench during games. I ask him why he does certain things. I don't think I'd like to play too long. I've often said I'd play until I'm 29 if I had what I wanted. But how do you know? At 29, I'd still like baseball. But 32–35 is long enough. I don't want to exhaust it. Then maybe I'd like to manage."

Suddenly Bench was in a hurry. He discarded his uniform and his cold drink and he headed for the shower. Later he dried himself and pulled on his bell-bottoms and his gaudy see-through body shirt.

"It's my folks' anniversary," he said, buttoning the last button. "We're having a house full of people. You know—weed your way through, put down some cake. All my folks will be there."

All his folks. Only a few years ago it seemed that most of the superstars existed without families, without roots, eager to gobble up all the goodies in the big leagues, reluctant to share what lay behind. The gentle, routine players like Ruben Amaro, Steve Hamilton, Ed Charles—they lived and breathed and had families. But the superstars only had flunkies who could get them a good deal on banlon golf shirts.

Johnny Bench's mother and father now operate the Poe Motel in the suburbs of Cincinnati. One of his two brothers works in town. So does his sister. And his grandmothers and aunts and uncles always seem to be flying in from Oklahoma.

"You'll see John looking around during the game to see who's here," Sparky Anderson said. "When he hits a homer, he'll look into the stands where Ted and Katie are sitting, to see if they're happy."

"We never had much," said Johnny Bench, rushing home to the family. "I can remember working in the fields, mowing lawns, paper route, anything to bring in some money. My parents worked hard for me. I'm glad to be close to them now."

Ernie Banks is a genius. He must be a genius because people have trouble understanding him. For almost 20 years he's been telling Chicago Cubs followers: "It's a great day for a ballgame." Except when there's a doubleheader. Then Ernie chirps, "Let's play four."

Ernie was chirping "Let's play four" on this steamy Sunday morning, despite the fact that his feet would be planted in the 110-degree turf, on and off for the next six hours. He was positively ecstatic when he saw an old acquaintance from New York. ("East Side, West Side, all around the town," Ernie sang.) Then the old acquaintance asked Ernie about Johnny Bench.

"Johnny Bench," Ernie intoned, spinning chatter off the top of his head. "Johnny Bench. Oh, yes. Johnny Bench is a Sagittarius. Did you know that? Born in December. Sagittarians are very goal-oriented. They see what they want, they do it. He's a leader. You can tell by looking at him. I've watched him. Every day he goes off to left field by himself before the game. To think. It's not that he doesn't want to talk to people. He just needs to get his thoughts together.

"He had that great year and he said to himself, 'What should I do now? What can I do for an encore?' I think it took him a year to rediscover himself."

I asked Ernie what sign he was born under. Naturally, it was Aquarius.

"Aquarius doesn't set goals," Ernie said. "When I hit the 47 homers in 1958, I didn't set a goal for next season. I just came out to see what would happen. But Sagittarians are different. Sagittarians tend to get tense when they don't reach their goals."

The bad year probably began with the good year. Bench hit 45 homers and drove in 148 runs, and he was voted Most Valuable Player as the Reds won the pennant in 1970. Single and attractive, he was in demand all over the world. He had his own television show, he had business deals, he had singing engagements.

"Twenty-two years old, flying from New York to Chicago to Pittsburgh to Tulsa, meeting the governors. Then the Bob Hope thing. He went to Vietnam. He met all the big people," Sparky Anderson capsulized.

Bench did half the things because they sounded exciting and half because he was asked. "Everybody has a just cause," Bench recalls. "I've always been hesitant to say no." So he didn't say no. He just kept going, all that winter of 1970–71, until suddenly it was time for spring training again.

"You're exhausted after a winter like that," Sparky said. "I don't care if you think you are—you are. It's not the baseball. It's the smiling."

Tired of smiling, late reporting to spring training, John rushed into 1971 swinging for the fences. He had to. There wasn't anybody else.

Bobby Tolan had torn up his ankle playing basketball in the winter, Lee May had a bad leg, and Tony Perez had a sore hand.

Boom. Bench had nine homers in April, 13 by the middle of May. He also had bad habits at the plate.

"He was trying to sweep the ball out of the ballpark instead of just meeting it with a good, compact short stroke like he had last year. Sure, he might get some home runs when the ball happens to be in the right spot, but he couldn't hit with any consistency with a swing like that," said Ted Kluszewski, the Reds' hitting coach, who used to hit a homer once in a while.

"I took too much for granted," Bench said. "People expect an awful lot of you when you have a season like I had in 1970. I'll probably never have another that great. I started pressing in 1971 and that made it worse."

The whole Reds team struggled all year, Bench included, and the fans began to boo their superstar on his way to .238 with 27 homers and 61 RBIs.

"Sure, they found out how to pitch to him," Anderson said. "Low and away, get him anxious on that slider. He wanted to pull it to left field. He was almost embarrassed sometimes. Sure, they booed him. The stars hear more than normal."

Anderson said he was never worried that Bench might be in a permanent slump. "He had to come back," the manager said. "He's too good a ballplayer. If they're gonna get to you, it's gonna be in your second year, not your fourth. He just made some mistakes in 1971, but it wasn't all his fault, either. The pitchers found how to pitch to him. Heck, I knew how to pitch to him. Just don't make a mistake!"

Toward the end of the season, Sparky didn't want to risk Bench carrying that slump into the winter. So he suggested something that Most Valuable Players don't usually do—a month or so in Florida, at the winter instructional league, where clubs send their promising young players who need to work on their skills.

"We didn't want him playing in the games," Sparky said. "We just wanted him to concentrate on the mental thing. We wanted him to watch films for 30 minutes a day, sit in that room and concentrate.

"We had this tremendous film of the great hitters—Ruth, Gehrig, Musial, Williams, and that little guy, Paul Waner. Then we had pictures of John. One thing we learned—they may all have different stances but all good hitters end up the same when they connect. John's swing was the same as theirs. I wanted him to see it. Once you see it, it's there, in your mind."

Bench says he didn't object when the Reds suggested he go to Florida. He says he found Lew Fonseca, the hitting instructor with the films, to be "a super guy." So Bench spent his mornings watching films and hitting against the machine. Then when the youngsters would play their winter league game, Bench would go play golf. After a few weeks of concentration, he began to enjoy a more leisurely winter than the previous one.

"I had my agency put a fee on my appearances," he said. "It was the only way. If they couldn't pay it, that solved the problem."

The Reds also concerned themselves with his business dealings, asking him to get rid of his share in an automobile agency in Dayton and a bowling alley in Cincinnati. Bench seemed to get more upset when they asked him to pare five pounds off his rugged 6'1" frame. "I don't have an ounce of fat on me," he bristled in December. "And you wonder how I could weigh 212—what I weighed in midseason of 1970—and do the job and now suddenly be overweight at 205."

He agreed that Joe Torre's fine season in 1971, after losing weight, probably was on the front office's mind. "They seemed to think the only reason Torre had such a great year was because he lost some weight," Bench argued. "They aren't taking into consideration the one thing Torre himself will tell you—getting away from catching to third base gave him the opportunity to think about his hitting. I'm sure losing the weight helped him. He was too heavy. But he wasn't built to carry the weight he was carrying. I don't think I am too heavy. But I am going to do what they say."

Bench lost the weight and seemingly lost the resentment by the time spring training opened in 1972.

"Last year John didn't want to be around people as much, because he was tired," Anderson said. "But this year he was glad to be around people again. I could see him talking to people in the stands, talking to kids."

Before John could test his new concentration during the season, the entire rhythm of baseball was thrown off by the first effective strike in major league history. The season was delayed as almost all the players stuck together, substitutes and superstars.

"I tried to tell people what we were after," Bench said. "But let's face it, the same people run the newspaper and the ballclub in Cincinnati. That hurt our coverage at home. But I could see why people in Cincinnati were mad. Cincinnati is traditionally the opening city, with brass bands and a sellout crowd. It's a prestigious thing—and we were taking it away from them."

The fans had heard Bench's casual suggestion that he might not tip his cap in 1972, after the way they booed him in 1971. So when the strike ended, and the Reds held a solemn and anticlimactic Opening Day, they booed their young catcher. But their biggest boos were reserved for Jim Merritt, the lefty pitcher who was struggling to stay in the major leagues and had acted as player representative during the strike.

The season started slowly for Bench, one hit for 22 at-bats—more boos, some nervous tension for his folks in the stands. (His mother came down with shingles.) With Joe Morgan on base all the time, with Bobby Tolan recovered, the pitchers couldn't fool around as much with Bench. He broke out with a cluster of home runs and, without attracting much attention, began tipping his cap again. All was right with Bench's world again.

The gloomy Jim Merritt didn't fare so well. With the boos ringing in his ears, he was trundled off to Indianapolis to try to regain his pitching form. And the new player representative was the Reds' busy young catcher. "They wanted me to," Bench said. "Nobody else wanted it. After Merritt, I could see why. I took it. It was a responsibility."

Even with the hitting problem in 1971, Bench's defense was better than ever. He improved his handling of low pitches, his one slight weakness of the past, and he learned even more about opposing hitters. He had never been hesitant to call the pitches, not from the first day he broke into the majors. Other players called him "the Little General," but they weren't smiling when he gave the orders.

Jim Maloney, a great fastball pitcher when his arm wasn't aching, once confessed: "I'm about 10 years older than Johnny. Yet he'll come out to the mound and chew me out as if I were a two-year-old. So help me, this kid coaches me. And I like it."

Everybody on the Reds liked the way Bench moved behind the plate. Sparky Anderson noted he had seen Bench break backward, out of his crouch to snare tiny popups about to spin to earth.

"I've never seen any catcher turn around and get those," Sparky marveled. "I don't know how he does it. He's got to be one of the top three catchers in baseball history. No, I don't mean in the future. I mean right now."

Bases loaded. Cubs leading, 5–0. Ferguson Jenkins, one of the best in the business, pitches low and away to Bench. Swinging strike. Seen from behind, Bench seems round-shouldered and ponderous, strength in his arms and shoulders, more Killebrew than Aaron. Then Jenkins works him inside, moving him back. Then low and outside again. Bench lunges, gets a piece of the ball, whistles a line drive down the left-field line but fading...fading...foul. A few steps down the line, Bench does a heavy two-step dance of despair at losing a grand-slam home run by so slight a margin. Back in the box he hunches over the plate, perhaps remembering the lesson of last year, the lunging for bad pitches. On the next pitch Ferguson Jenkins catches the plate, low and away, for called strike three. The Reds never threaten again.

"Before the game I was kidding John about all his power," Jenkins said, calm after an easy victory. "I asked him if he was saving it for Sunday. I thought of that when he hit that foul homer. But I didn't remind him of it. Not while he was batting. A guy like that, he's liable to wax you and then laugh at you around the bases."

What did Jenkins think about that bad year in 1971?

"It's like a cycle," he said. "Forty-five homers, hitting a lot of fastballs. Then last year they were giving him outside pitches and he went for them. Now he's switched bats and he leans over the plate more. He adjusted to the pitchers. Now I've got to adjust to him. I'm not going to challenge his strength. Low and away. Sliders. But he's going to wax you a lot of times anyway."

Jim LaBarbara is a disc jockey who used to sneak some vintage Beatles and angelic Joni Mitchell in between the Top 40 glop. Once in a while he'd ask a few intelligent questions of a guest musician. Like, he was the best AM disc jockey in the Ohio Valley. Then one day he was rapping about the Neil Diamond record about the frog who dreamed he was a prince—you know, about a guy who wants to be in one place but instead is in another. A few weeks later Jim LaBarbara moved from Cincinnati to Denver.

"Me and John lived in the same apartment building," LaBarbara said over the telephone. "John would say to me, 'Let's go to the hospital and talk to the kids.' John would always do stuff like that, nobody heard about it. Then John had that dynamite year and people said, 'John's not the same. John's changed.' But John didn't change.

"But it was tough. We'd go places and people would get on John. One time this old drunk came up and poked John in the chest and said, 'You lost the World Series for us.' John didn't say much. He just kept it inside.

"When things were going bad in 1971, John used to come to the studio while I was on. We'd sit and talk about records. I'd think to myself, 'Wow, here is this guy, Most Valuable Player, and he doesn't want to talk about himself, he wants to talk about music.' John is really into lyrics. He listens to what the people are saying.

"When the fans really got on him last year he stopped coming around to the studio. He said people got down on him when they heard he was out in L.A. with Chuck Connors, things like that. He didn't go out as much. He backed off. But we'd go to the Inner Circle on Vine Street where he made his singing debut, or another rock place out by the university. The people know John there. They don't hassle him.

"We used to double-date a lot. John was always nice to girls. I've seen ballplayers tell a girl to get lost just because she wasn't really pretty. But John would talk with girls that definitely were not pretty. He likes to get to know people.

"John keeps his friends, too. Even girls he used to date. One girl he knew, I ran into her, said John still called once in a while to see how she was. And his girlfriends are all intelligent. John might be taking out some chick in Hollywood, then he comes back to Cincinnati and takes out a chick who works in an office, but I don't think he treats them any different.

"I think he's really enjoying life now. I talked to him one time about growing up. I asked him didn't he have dates back home in Oklahoma. He said he was too busy working. I asked him didn't he have dates in the minor leagues, in Buffalo. He said he didn't have enough money.

"Now he's having a ball. But he's got to be careful. One time at a party somebody handed him a joint [marijuana]. In a situation like that, a young guy might be tempted to take a few puffs to show he's part of the crowd. But not John. He handed it back. He's really down on drugs.

"Another time somebody put him down because he had short hair. I've got long hair and a beard, you know. John's got to keep his hair short because of the army. John said the guy shouldn't judge people on the basis of their appearance. The guy apologized.

"I know John looks out for his future. He talked to me one time about Randy Hundley, who was the premier catcher in John's opinion, before he got hurt. John said the same thing could happen to him any time. You never know. John often talks about retiring when he's 30. I know he'd like to settle down and get married."

John Bench rushed into the clubhouse for the Sunday double-header, after spending the morning at a reserve meeting. He took batting practice and then spotted his persistent visitor lurking near his locker. (The locker next to Bench is empty, to catch the overflow of mail and visitors.) Bench motioned to a chair in the empty locker.

The subject was John's social life.

"The players accept me. I'm single. Other guys would like to be able to do the things I do. But they're married. They're tied down to a job and family in the off-season. Yes, I think about marriage. I think I've got a mental picture of what I want. Sometimes I wonder if I've been spoiled. I know I'd like to get married eventually."

In the old days, it used to seem big news when a handsome young superstar was also a bachelor, a target for single girls everywhere. But maybe things have changed in the '70s. "Maybe 10 years ago, I can't remember, families expected early marriage for their daughters," Bench said. "But now there are so many divorces. Maybe people don't expect girls to marry so young anymore. It isn't a problem for me."

He started talking about his condominium on Mount Adams, overlooking the Ohio River, a touch of San Francisco in the Ohio Valley, with quaint homes nestling against modernistic, with old-generation ethnic people rubbing elbows with the elegant chic of Cincinnati, with leather shops and neighborhood groceries side by side.

John said he lives in a three-story building. When I asked which floor, his eyes opened a trifle wider. "All three," he said. "I've got two baths, seven rooms."

He said he likes to cook steak or bacon and eggs but noted, "I'm not much for soufflés or casseroles. Lots of times I'll eat at Pia's. That's Pia Battaglia; she's got a grocery store near my house. I'll go over in the morning and she'll insist on fixing me a meal. She always gives me more than I can handle. Al Battaglia, he was our trainer last year, he'll call me when I've got to get up early for reserves or catch a plane. They really take care of me. Great people."

Then we got into the music. John has sung in Las Vegas and Cincinnati, and people say he'd rather have a singing career than be a manager. "I like all kinds of music, from country and western to rock. I saw *Jesus Christ, Superstar* in New York. I liked it a lot. I like the Carpenters, Charlie Pride, Conway Twitty, Jerry Lee Lewis, Don McLean, James Taylor, Carole King. All kinds of pop stuff. I would guess, however, that my favorite artist is Bobby Goldsboro. Bobby is a friend of mine."

I mentioned a song by Bobby Goldsboro that I like. Bench smiled in recognition and started singing in a husky voice.

> "I can imagine myself as a gypsy,
> a seeker of fortunes on a far-away shore,
> having some fun with golden girls in the sand,
> chasing the sun through invisible lands,
> leaving the straight life behind...."

He sang another verse, his face with a serious expression, his mind deep into the words, not looking around for attention, just singing, it was obvious, because he liked it.

"Ray Stevens had a record I liked called *Everything Is Beautiful*. It gave me a good feeling. I use it a lot when I'm making a speech somewhere. He had another one called *Hey, Mr. Businessman*, where he questions the way people behave. I feel the same way. There's a lot of sham in the world. I listen to the politicians at these conventions, I wonder if the people really have a choice. I always say what I believe. But are the candidates telling the truth? Even if they are, what can they do about it with this counterbalance system?

"I think a lot about Congress and the Supreme Court. One thing that's really got me is this Supreme Court decision abolishing the death penalty. Take somebody like Sirhan Sirhan. He just wiped out an idol of millions of people—but now the Supreme Court says we shouldn't wipe him out. I'm really hipped on the subject. Suppose you rob some helpless person. Now you can kill him and the law won't kill you. Sometimes I think you should take all the murderers and just lock 'em up in a room and let 'em have it. I really do."

I made a few preliminary arguments against the death penalty and Bench seemed willing to listen to my side of the issue. But a clatter of spikes told him that it was time for the team to begin infield practice. So he got up from his chair, picked up his mitt, and said good-bye.

"Did you get enough?" he said, scrutinizing me again, I thought, the way he might scrutinize a pitcher who was trying to last the nine innings but whose arm was beginning to tire.

The doubleheader went on and on. The Reds lost the opener and Sparky Anderson rested Bench in the second game, only the third game he'd missed by midseason. But without Bench the Reds lacked cohesion. They missed his bat and they missed his charisma. The Reds lost the second game even worse. Around the seventh inning I decided I'd had enough of Cincinnati on this steamy summer weekend, knowing that Bench had a family outing on Sunday evening and would not feel like talking after a double loss. So I headed across the river again, thinking about this young man who sang a song with one breath and executed a room full of murderers with the next, and then could rush home to visit his family in the evening.

Earl Lawson, *The Sporting News*

PLAYER OF THE YEAR AWARD FOR HOUSE OF MORGAN

When the Mighty Mite arrived in Cincinnati for the 1972 season, no one could have possibly known the effect he would have on the Reds. Unheralded in Houston, Joe Morgan exploded with the Reds and over the next six seasons he was the catalyst that helped Cincinnati win four division titles, three pennants, and two world championships. Baseball writers bestowed back-to-back MVP awards on Morgan in 1975 and 1976, but it could have been three or four. Earl Lawson profiled Morgan for The Sporting News *on January 3, 1976.*

Joe Morgan already has an architect designing a home he plans to have built during the 1976 season.

"And," said Joe, "it's beginning to look as if I'm going to have to tell him to make some changes in the original plans I outlined."

The house plan calls for a music room.

"That room will have to be enlarged," said Joe, "so I can display all of the trophies that I'm accumulating this year."

Morgan's latest award honors him as The Sporting News Major League Player of the Year.

Twice during the regular season, Morgan, the Reds' All-Star second baseman, was named the National League's Player of the Month.

Shortly before Morgan delivered the game-winning hit in the seventh game of the World Series with the Red Sox to give the Reds their first world championship in 35 years, Joe was voted The Sporting News National League Player of the Year.

Then came the National League's Most Valuable Player award.

Shortly thereafter Morgan learned that he had been voted a Gold Glove as a member of The Sporting News NL All-Star Fielding Team for the third straight year.

"And now the major leagues' Player of the Year....wow," exclaimed Morgan.

Joe had just entered his Oakland home after playing three sets of tennis when he received the telephone call informing him of his latest honor.

"You know," he said, "I was so hopped up about our winning the World Series that it was just a couple of weeks ago that I began realizing just how much the individual awards I'm collecting mean to me."

For instance, Morgan is only the fourth second baseman to win the National League's Most Valuable Player award.

The three others were Rogers Hornsby, Jackie Robinson, and Frankie Frisch.

"And," pointed out Morgan, "since all three are in the Hall of Fame, winning that MVP award puts me in pretty select company.

"And Player of the Year in the majors! Without knowing, I'll bet not too many second basemen have been voted that award."

The answer—one, Bill Mazeroski in 1960.

"You know," mused Joe, "I'd like to take a little time right now to offer thanks to a few people who have given me a lot of help along the way...people who have done a lot to make it possible for me to win the awards that have been coming my way."

There's the Houston club, for example.

"I'm indebted to the Astros because they gave me the chance to play in the majors when other clubs thought I was too small to make the grade," said Morgan.

Then, there was Nellie Fox, who died only recently, a victim of cancer.

Nellie, like Morgan, was small of stature, but it didn't prevent him from winning the American League Most Valuable Player award as a second baseman for the pennant-winning White Sox of 1959.

"Fox exerted a great influence on me when he was a coach and I was a player at Houston," said Joe. "He impressed upon me the fact that a player should never permit a batting slump to affect his fielding."

Nellie stressed the point that a great play in the field often can compensate for the hit a slump-ridden player doesn't get with a runner in scoring position.

"I talked with Nellie the day before he died," recalled Morgan. "All he talked about was how happy he was for me. And here was a guy dying of cancer. Tells you a lot about him, huh?"

Jimmy Adair was another coach at Houston during Morgan's years with the Astros.

"Just give your best all the time you're in a game," Adair would tell Joe. "Do that and there'll never be a reason for you to hang your head in shame, even if you make an error that costs your team a victory."

Morgan recalled the year 1968 when he sat out most of the season after suffering a crippling knee injury during a second-base collision with Tommie Agee, then a member of the Mets.

"I learned a lot just sitting on the bench and in the stands watching games," recalled Joe.

Sitting there, Morgan realized that he had been squandering a God-given talent—his speed.

"I realized," said Joe, "that old ballparks were being replaced by new and larger ballparks...that AstroTurf was fast replacing natural grass.

"I began to realize," said Joe, "larger ballparks would mean fewer home-run hitters, that there was a bright future for the ballplayers with speed and the ability to make contact with pitches."

This past season, Morgan batted .327, drew 132 walks, hit 17 homers, and drove home 94 runs.

"There's one of my 1975 statistics that isn't mentioned very much," said Joe, "but it's one of which I'm particularly proud."

The statistics?

"Among players with a minimum of 502 plate appearances," said Joe, "I hit into the fewest double plays—three."

And, as any pitcher will quickly tell you, the double play is the best play in baseball...a real rally stopper.

Morgan's also proud of the 67 bases he stole in 77 attempts.

"You steal a base," he pointed out, "and a sacrifice bunt isn't needed to put you in scoring position. You save your club an out."

Morgan admitted that his .327 batting mark surprised him.

"The number of times I walk [132 this past season] I didn't think it would be possible for me to bat that high since I average only three and a half official trips to the plate," he said.

Shortly after the Christmas holidays, Morgan will begin strenuous daily workouts to prepare for spring training.

"Getting into the best shape possible...that's the key to having a good season," said Morgan. "I'll try, but I don't think I can report this spring in any better physical condition than last year."

As for the 1978 season?

"I'm not predicting I'll top my .327 average," said Joe, "but I'm counting on hitting 20 or more homers and driving home 100 or more runs."

He's also counting on playing on another world championship team.

"It's nice being recognized everywhere you go," he said.

It's nice, too, knowing you're in demand for personal appearances.

"I've tried to keep these at a minimum, though, because I like to spend as much time as possible during the off-season with my family and friends," said Joe.

"But, I'll be on hand for the writers' dinners in New York, St. Louis, and Chicago. I'll be in Cincinnati for the old timers dinner, too.

"Oh yeah," he added, "I'll be one of the 10 Reds who'll compete in the super team event in Hawaii in February.

"We'll compete against 10 players from the Red Sox," he explained. "Then the winner will compete against the team that wins a matchup of the Super Bowl contestants."

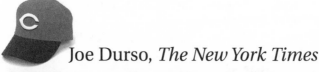

Joe Durso, *The New York Times*

THE PAINFUL COLLAR OF PETE ROSE

It would be a safe bet to assume that no other modern ballplayer has had as many things written about him as Pete Rose. The player who would "walk through hell in a gasoline suit to keep playing baseball" loved his time on the diamond as much as anyone who ever put on a baseball cap and spikes. But in many ways he remains as much of an enigma in the public's eye today as he was when he was running nonstop in ballparks around the country. Joe Durso covered Rose's 44-game hitting streak in 1978 for The New York Times.

"When my hitting streak was ended," he was saying the other day, "I felt terrible. I felt as though I'd lost my best friend."

Joe DiMaggio sat back in his chair and remembered his "best friend" of 37 years ago: 223 times at bat, 91 hits, 15 home runs, and an average of .408. Also, 56 straight games, the hitting streak they said would never be broken. No wonder he felt as though he had lost his best friend.

When Pete Rose passed 38 straight games a couple of weeks ago, setting a modern record for the National League, he received a telegram for Joe DiMaggio that read: "Congratulations and good luck."

"I didn't particularly want him to break my record," Joe was saying. "I was wishing him well for the opportunity he had. I have nothing but admiration for this man to go as far as he's gone."

Then Pete Rose was streaking past 39 straight, taking aim on DiMaggio's best friend and saying: "I got half a building built. Got to go on to the rest of it now. But it wouldn't be the end of the world if I went 0-for-4."

"He's got the bat," Joe D. observed with absolute logic. "He's going to have to do it."

So last Tuesday night in Atlanta, in the same stadium where Henry Aaron broke Babe Ruth's home-run record four years ago, Pete Rose went 0-for-4.

Batting against a rookie left-hander named Larry McWilliams, he walked on a 3–2 pitch in the first inning, hit a line drive that the pitcher

46

speared in the second, and grounded out to shortstop in the fifth. Then, swinging against an experienced, bearded right-hander, Gene Garber, he lined out to third base (into a double play) in the seventh and struck out on a 2–2 changeup in the ninth—ending the game and the streak at 44 games.

Roses for Rose

When it was over, Pete Rose received a standing ovation and a bouquet of roses from the Atlanta Braves. But the thing he will remember most about the night of August 1, 1978, is the collar he got from McWilliams and Garber: 0-for-4.

But Pete Rose, the most combative of baseball players, who asks no quarter and gives none, stepped out of character in a moment of disappointment or pique and said:

"Garber was pitching like it was the seventh game of the World Series. He had a 16–4 lead. I'm not saying anything about him bearing down. I just said he should challenge somebody. I had one pitch to swing at that was a strike. Most pitchers in baseball just challenge a guy in that situation. He was just trying to in-and-out, up-and-down you."

"I wanted his streak to continue," replied Garber, a 31-year-old Pennsylvanian with a wicked sidearm whip, "but I wanted to get him out, too. That's what I get paid to do. That's the way I always pitch. I had an idea he was hitting like it was the ninth inning of the World Series. The one thing I didn't want to do was end the streak with a walk."

"If Phil Niekro had been pitching and I got five pitches," Pete persisted, "I guarantee you three would have been fastballs. I wouldn't have seen the knuckleball, his best pitch."

One for the Home Folks

Well, he may have been right about that. The night before, Niekro had fed Pete a fastball in the sixth inning, and Pete obliged by bouncing it past the second baseman for a single. But he was wrong if he thought that was the way for Niekro to "challenge" him or anybody else. Niekro challenges you with the knuckler; he mixes in an occasional fastball to break the spell, not to break the streak.

Pete Rose can be forgiven for his disappointment; he has been hustling for the Cincinnati Reds for 16 rousing summers. But Gene Garber also struck out Junior Kennedy and Vic Correll in the ninth inning, and he owed Pete nothing. The guessing game between pitcher and batter is just that, a guessing game.

The trouble is that we have all grown record-crazy in sports. Performance pays big, and records glamorize performance—for the individual and the business both.

Maybe baseball owes Pete Rose a vote of thanks, or maybe the Cincinnati Reds owe him a fat new contract when his old one runs out this winter.

When he brought his streak to Philadelphia, attendance jumped by 11,000 a game. In New York, it soared 100 percent. In Atlanta, he drew 45,007 when he tied Willie Keeler's National League record at 44 games the night before, about 32,000 above average.

But records should not be staged for promotional pull, Nielsen ratings, or box-office zing. They become gimmicks, bigger than the competition that makes a sporting event work. You tamper with the schedule or the setting, you set a record and lose a value.

Remember three months ago, when Pete Rose was closing in on his 3,000th hit? His manager, Sparky Anderson, a passionate and decent man, confessed that there was "no way" he would permit Rose to make it in New York or anywhere but before the folks back home in Cincinnati. Even if the game in New York was at stake? Even then, he said, sticking to his emotional guns.

For that indiscretion, he got a fast phone call from Chub Feeney, president of the National League. But Pete got the big hit back home.

Even Henry Aaron's pursuit of Babe Ruth was embroiled by home-town hype. Henry hit number 714 in Cincinnati on Opening Day of 1974, which posed a problem for his team, the Atlanta Braves: they had two more games in Cincinnati before returning home. So they benched the best home-run hitter in baseball, fearful that he might just tag another.

The commissioner, Bowie Kuhn, stepped in that time, and rightfully so. He ordered the Braves to play Aaron because the integrity of the game was at stake. So, after sitting out one game, he returned to the lineup, took two called third strikes and grounded out to third base before leaving in the seventh inning. Later, he bristled when people asked if he had been trying his best. But safely back home in Atlanta the next night, on national television, he creamed the first pitch thrown over the plate.

The point of any record should be one thing: excellence. That is what Pete Rose has pursued for 16 summers. That was what Gene Garber was pursuing on the night of August 1, 1978.

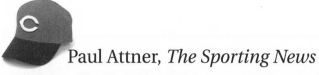

Paul Attner, *The Sporting News*

THE RECORD AND ROSE

It is the record, Rose's record. Baseball's all-time hit king broke Ty Cobb's record for career hits on September 11, 1985, when he singled off San Diego's Eric Show. Rose had tied the record three days earlier at Chicago's Wrigley Field with a single off the Cubs' Reggie Patterson. The Sporting News' Paul Attner wrote the following article about Rose's pursuit of the hit record. Because the September 8 game against the Cubs was eventually called due to darkness, Rose was able to break the record in Cincinnati. This article appeared in the magazine's September 16, 1985, edition.

As the fans in Wrigley Field stood and the chants of "Pete! Pete!" began, Pete Rose set up slowly in the batter's box. On the mound, Reggie Patterson, who had been in the minors just five days earlier, looked in for his sign.

Earlier on the afternoon of September 8, Rose had lined a first-inning single off the Chicago Cubs right-hander to pull within one of Ty Cobb's all-time major league hits record. Mark it down, Rose had said the previous day. If he got a hit the first time up, "I may not have to carry my bat" to the plate after that. His own adrenalin—and the excitement of the fans—would be enough to pull him to the record.

In the third inning, Rose had grounded weakly to second, driving in a run for the Cincinnati Reds. Still, the Wrigley fans remained optimistic. Now it was the fifth inning and the electricity filled the old park, shaking the ivy lining the outfield wall.

"Pete! Pete! Pete!" the 28,269 fans chanted. In the batter's box, Rose heard the cheers. He tapped his helmet and crouched low in that familiar coiled stance.

Ten months earlier, the lanky Patterson had been shot in the neck during a robbery while in Caracas, Venezuela, to play winter ball. The doctors had warned him he might never pitch again. Now, he was on the brink of being yanked into baseball history. Even though it suddenly seemed he was on the visiting team and the man at the plate was the hometown hero, he kept telling himself this was "just another batter in just another game."

Rose took the first two pitches, both screwballs, both strikes. The fans groaned, but nobody was sitting down. Patterson then wasted two one-bounce pitches to even the count. The fifth pitch was another ball, just outside.

"I wasn't going to walk him," Patterson said later. The crowd raised the noise level even higher.

Rose, who already had delivered two hits off Patterson in this three-game weekend series, was sure "I could get the ball into play" off the young pitcher. He figured fastball. Patterson threw a screwball, but to Rose it looked like a heater, a not very effective heater. And even at age 44, after almost 23 seasons, Peter Edward Rose can still turn an average pitch into a hit.

He exploded from his coil, lashing out with his black bat, the one imprinted with "PR—4,192," and lined the ball to right center for a clean single. The ultimate singles hitter in major league history had tied Ty Cobb's record in the most appropriate fashion possible. How many of his other 4,191 hits had looked just the same? But to Rose and the ecstatic throng in Wrigley Field, this line drive was as magnificent as any mighty homer they had ever witnessed.

As Rose stood on first, the cheering continued in ever-increasing waves for two minutes. Rose wasn't sure what to do; he finally raised a finger in the air and doffed his batting helmet. "Don't move," said first baseman Leon Durham. "I want to get some national television exposure." In right field, Keith Moreland applauded. Patterson began to walk over to shake Rose's hand, then thought better of it and returned to the mound.

"It was just another base hit," said Patterson, who was four years old when Rose was a Reds rookie in 1963. But Patterson, the newest addition to baseball trivia, finally broke down and admitted he was excited, calling Rose "the greatest player to ever play." If he could, he said he would like to talk to Rose and tell him, "Way to hit the ball."

Rose, of course, still had some unfinished business. He would get up twice more this day. He bounced to shortstop off Lary Sorensen in the seventh inning and, after a rain delay of more than two hours, he struck out in the ninth against Lee Smith with two men on base.

That meant he had to travel back to Cincinnati, where the Reds began a nine-game home stand September 9, to break Cobb's mark. But even his hometown fans couldn't exceed the enthusiasm of the Chicago crowd; nor could the drama be more memorable than on the afternoon at Wrigley Field when one of baseball's most revered and longest lasting (57 years since Cobb's retirement in 1928) records was equaled.

The day and the moment were full of ironies. Rose, the most prolific switch-hitter in baseball history, has been starting only against right-handed pitching this season. And with left-hander Steve Trout scheduled to hurl for the Cubs, the Reds' manager had penciled in Tony Perez at first base. But Trout fell off his bicycle the night before, suffered a bruised shoulder and elbow, and had to be scratched. Two hours before the game, Rose learned that Patterson was to start, so he made the lineup switch and took out Perez.

But there wasn't time either to stop his family from returning to Cincinnati or to alert owner Marge Schott that she should fly to Chicago. So Rose found himself in a dilemma: Should he ignore the urgings of the fans and the presence of an ever-increasing press corps and hold back until he could return on Monday to Cincinnati, where Schott had said she wanted the record to fall? Or should he go all out, as usual?

"I had 30,000 people yelling here," he said, "and one lady [Schott] sitting back in Cincinnati kicking her dog [a St. Bernard named Schottzie] every time I got a hit." (Mrs. Schott heard the game on a portable radio while attending the Cincinnati-Seattle NFL opener in Cincinnati.)

His players gave unsolicited advice. After the first hit, Dave Parker kept walking by in the dugout, asking, "What are you doing? Don't do it, don't do it." Dave Concepcion told him to "take his batting glove and go watch the game on television."

But Rose, badgered for days about where he wanted to get the hit, could respond in only one way. He had never held back in his career, whether in a meaningless exhibition or an All-Star Game, and he couldn't start now. Besides, he still thinks the Reds have a chance to win the National League West and he wasn't about to hurt the team with a halfhearted try.

"You've got to try to win," he said. "I was just going up there and trying to get base hits."

But Schott, who was calling frantically from Cincinnati during the rain delay, trying to talk to Reds officials in Chicago, wasn't appeased by Rose's attitude. "The fans in Cincinnati deserved to see the record tied and broken," she declared. "Pete shouldn't have started today in Chicago. No one would have complained."

The rain delay, which temporarily stopped the game in the bottom of the eighth, added more irony to the already striking afternoon. When play resumed, the Reds tied the game at 5-all in the ninth. After the Cubs were retired, and with darkness engulfing the field, the umpires suspended the game. In any other major league park, play would have continued. But at Wrigley, without lights, Rose would get no more chances.

The game will be recorded as a tie and all statistical results are official. But if the outcome later has a bearing on the pennant race, the game would be replayed in its entirety, owing to a rule that applies only to Chicago's Wrigley Field. In the last meeting of the season between two clubs there (this was the Reds' last visit), a game called because of darkness is complete and official. So hit number 4,191 arrived in a game that will never have a winner.

Rose wasn't worrying about such statistical quirks, not with his name already next to Cobb's in the record book. "This is a special day," he said. "It's got to be the biggest individual thing to ever happen to anybody."

Once Manager Rose settled on first baseman Rose as a starter this season, it was only a matter of time before Cobb's record would fall. Rose knew it.

"There's no pressure," he said, "because there's no time constraint. Now if this was the last game of the season and I wasn't going to play next year, it would be a different matter."

Instead, Rose orchestrated the chase into a season-long media event. Few athletes have ever cooperated more freely with the press, and certainly few public figures have ever handled such an ongoing event so well. Of course, Rose long ago realized how he could turn this exposure into dollars and cents. With all the T-shirts, posters, coins, and books marking his quest, he'll need a Brinks truck to haul away his loot.

But don't expect Rose to become too analytical about his accomplishment. He isn't much for philosophical insight. It's always been a simple game for him. "You play as hard as you can and you play to win every time out." Everything else is superfluous.

That's why Cobb has always been special to Rose. Cobb also played hard and played to win. "I've dreamed about him," Rose said. But Cobb died two months after Rose signed his first pro contract, and the two never met. Instead, he's had to rely on the recollections of old-time players to get to know his hero.

"There's no doubt he is the greatest hitter ever to live, based on his average," said Rose. "I wish I could have seen him play."

Both men had comparable, massive egos, but Cobb ended his illustrious career without many friends among his peers or in the stands. Rose, who once earned the wrath of fans with his hell-bent style, has become a favorite in his final years. And players can hardly question his devotion or love for the game. Nobody on the Reds, for example, takes more batting practice than Rose, who claims he gets sluggish from even one day away from his beloved bats.

Nor can they have anything but envy for his numbers. Cobb, of course, has the ultimate numbers: 12 batting titles, .367 career average, 2,245 runs, 892 stolen bases. But Rose has been dazzling in his own right: most at-bats (13,763), most games played (3,474), most 200-hit seasons (10), most winning games (1,940), and, as he candidly points out, most outs.

Like Cobb, Rose was no teenage phenom. The hometown Reds signed him in 1960 as a courtesy. Three years later, after catching the eye of manager Fred Hutchinson, he surprised even himself by surviving spring training, where Mickey Mantle and Whitey Ford had mocked his enthusiasm by calling him "Charlie Hustle."

Rose has the physique of a home-run hitter, but he decided long ago his future would be built on a foundation of singles. He walked on his first major league at-bat, then went hitless the next 12 trips before lashing a triple off Bob Friend.

He would up winning the NL Rookie of the Year award. Later would come three batting titles, the 1975 NL Most Valuable Player award, an NL record 44-game hitting streak in 1978, and 17 All-Star selections. Free agency made him rich, but his heart always was in Cincinnati, which made last year's return to the city as player/manager after a six-season absence so touching and so fitting.

He's proven to be a fine manager, but that shouldn't be surprising. He always has had a mind for the game; it's been his whole life. Even now, with gray-streaked hair and a slightly bulging midsection, he maintains a little-boy affection for the sport. He is a throwback caught up in a modern era. Teammates go home and read the stock market reports; Rose goes home and watches other games on his satellite TV hookup.

He's also one of the game's biggest bargains. At a mere $250,000, his salary is puny in this era of the $1 million utility player. No wonder Charlie Hustle was hustling himself a raise from Schott in the days before tying Cobb.

"I'm one of the lowest paid players on this team," he said. "They got me cheap. But I think I've earned a raise." That's right, Rose wants to go through season number 24 to put some distance between him and Cobb.

Manager Rose has helped straighten out a tumbling franchise, turning the Reds into contenders. Indeed, Rose's refusal to rule out a possible pennant for his club kept interfering those final days with the Cobb quest. Writers couldn't understand why Rose wouldn't play every day; Rose kept explaining that he has spent the season sitting out against left-handers, and he wasn't about to alter his approach now, Cobb or no Cobb.

Still, despite Rose's stubbornness, and his desire to tie and surpass Cobb in Cincinnati, the Cubs' injury-depleted pitching staff all but forced him to make a move in Chicago.

"It's like spending a day in the American Association," said one writer about the Chicago staff. In the opening game of the series, September 6, the Cubs started Derek Botelho, appearing in only his seventh game after spending much of the season in the minors.

Even though Rose protested that he has trouble with pitchers he has never previously faced, he wiped out a first-inning strikeout by driving a Botelho fastball into the right-field stands in the second inning for only his second homer of the year (number 160 of his career). The fans cheered so long that he finally had to come to the top step of the dugout and wave.

"That [a curtain call] has never happened to me before," said Rose, unintentionally pointing out one of the burdens of hitting singles for a career. Wrigley fans usually toss back enemy home runs out of disdain; this time, applause or not, the ball stayed in the crowd.

After grounding out against young Jon Perlman, who was appearing in his first game of the season, Rose hit Patterson's first pitch to right center in the sixth for his second hit of the day. Then in the ninth against Ron Meridith, another recent minor leaguer, he struck out.

"I'll try to go 5-for-5 tomorrow," said Rose, who then was at 4,189 career hits. "But there is no doubt the record will come."

Nothing could dampen his enthusiasm, not even the fact his name had come up during the drug trial in Pittsburgh. "I thought I was vindicated with that [taking pills] in 1981," he said. "But I don't see why all of baseball should be smeared by what's going on there. I bet I've got a bigger crowd [of media] than they have in Pittsburgh. This is like the World Series."

The size of the press corps increased sharply for the Saturday game, September 7. The Cubs started Dennis Eckersley, who was coming back after an arm problem. Rose expected to get a couple of hits, but he couldn't solve Eckersley or the other three Chicago pitchers. He went 0-for-4 even though he lined a ball sharply in the sixth. Unfortunately, it was caught by another minor league pitching import, Jay Baller, who had no other choice since the ball was headed for his midsection.

"The ball caught him," said Rose, who could only laugh about the play. Before the game, he wasn't smiling. He had been sick to his stomach, but not from butterflies. Instead, he had become dehydrated from a workout in the humid, hot weather and nearly passed out until he took a cold shower. "My breakfast didn't taste as good the second time," he quipped.

Still, he maintained that the only pressure he felt was at night, when he tried to sleep. "I had to unplug my phone to get some rest," he said.

Sunday, of course, was a different story. For a while, it seemed he would even break the record. But Sorensen made a good pitch to get him out in the seventh and Smith proved too much in the ninth-inning dusk.

"Petey [his 15-year-old son] asked me if it was tough to see," said Rose. "I told him the last pitch from Smith [a swinging strike] sounded like a strike so I swung at it."

As usual, Rose had a sound reason for wanting to break the record in Chicago. "I'd rather tie and break it [here]," he said, "rather than go up in an airplane. That hasn't been the nicest way to travel the last month."

Rose flew safely to Cincinnati, but he left behind unforgettable history. "All I ever wanted to do is win games, get more hits, and score more runs [than anyone else]," he said. "Two out of three ain't bad."

Oh, yes, his next goal is to break the all-time record for runs scored. Three out of three is even better.

Daniel G. Habib, *Sports Illustrated*

JUNIOR'S FEELING GOOD

The father-son tandem has spanned two generations, their impact on the Reds unmistakable. Griffeys Sr. and Jr. both brought different aspects of the game to Cincinnati; but it is their bond to one another and the Reds that has made them special to the game. Senior added the speed and defense element to the Reds' 1975–76 world championship teams, Junior was hailed as the best player in baseball for several years. Father and son, and for two years in Seattle, teammates. Sports Illustrated *ran Daniel G. Habib's article on Junior in its June 14, 2004, issue.*

The way Junior saw it, the Mayor owed him a watch. "A Rolex," Junior said, "and not a New York City Rolex, either. I want to see the serial numbers." On a recent Friday night in Montreal, Sean Casey, the earnest Cincinnati Reds first baseman with the glad-handing chumminess of a small-town politician, had just finished smacking a single, two doubles, and a home run in five at-bats, boosting his batting average to .390. Ken Griffey Jr., Cincinnati's center fielder and, for the preceding month, its cleanup hitter behind Casey, reasoned that some of the credit belonged to him. "Just trying to let him know I'm protecting him, like the offensive line with the running back," said Griffey, who that night had hit his 493rd career home run, tying Lou Gehrig for 20th all time. "I figured out how I'll get [the watch], too. When we get home, I'll hold his car hostage. He always leaves his keys out in the open." Once more, Griffey crowed in Casey's direction, over the gaggle of reporters in a semicircle at the Mayor's locker. "A Rolex." Replied Casey, "A Timex, maybe."

Griffey, 34, adores this badinage. Though he stands on the verge of a milestone—after a pair of home runs on Sunday, he needed only two more to become the 20th player to crack 500 for his career—he thrills most to this role: the merry fraternity brother. He lards the idle hours before ballgames with jokes and quips, clowning and trash-talking with his teammates. Having just arrived at Olympic Stadium long before a Sunday matinee against the Montreal Expos, stripped down to a T-shirt but still wearing his dress slacks and shoes, he roams the clubhouse berating Michael Vassallo, the Reds' assistant director of media relations. "Vassallo? Where are the f—— clips? Where are those clips?" he demands in a loud voice, asking for the packet of the previous day's newspaper coverage of the team, which he actually has scant interest in reading. Approached by second baseman D'Angelo Jimenez with a baseball to sign, Griffey groans. "Again? Another one?"

"It's a team ball," a sheepish Jimenez says, pointing out the other autographs on it. Griffey signs it, then throws it at Jimenez's chest.

Griffey has had little chance to play this part since leaving the Seattle Mariners four years ago. When he joined the Reds in February 2000, after orchestrating a five-player trade to the city in which he had grown up and then accepting a below-market contract for $116.5 million over nine years, Griffey was the game's most complete and popular player. An elegant and graceful center fielder, he had won a Gold Glove and was voted a starter in the All-Star Game in each year of the 1990s; a lethal power hitter with hands as fast as a whiplash, he hit 382 home runs during the decade. By the heady arithmetic of projection, he was to eclipse Hank Aaron's home-run record of 755 shortly after turning 40. Fitted quickly with the mantle of the best player in the game, he grew to be gargantuan in stature.

"It was a circus," Casey says of Griffey's debut season with the Reds. "I didn't know if it was baseball or Barnum & Bailey. From the cameras on the first day of spring training, it never stopped, all year long. We looked at him like, 'Whoa, that's Ken Griffey Jr.,' and he looked at us and didn't know us. It was uncomfortable on both sides."

The marriage, of course, soured quickly, as Griffey succumbed to a series of freakish injuries—torn hamstrings and knee and ankle tendons, a dislocated shoulder—and the Reds lurched below .500, never a contender. Desperate to dump his contract, Cincinnati had him traded to the San Diego Padres before the 2003 season for third baseman Phil Nevin, but Nevin exercised his no-trade clause and blocked the deal. Coming into this season, Griffey had appeared in fewer than half of the Reds' games over the past three years. It is hard to say which is more improbable now: that the Reds, stripped down and sold for parts at last July's trade deadline, were 34–22 and two games up in the National League Central at week's end, or that Griffey, after seven months of rehabilitation from shoulder and ankle surgeries, was at last healthy. Though his .257 batting average and .359 on-base percentage are mediocre, he continues to hit for power, and it struck the ear as odd to hear Griffey liken himself, even in jest, to an offensive lineman, a faceless worker bee. Casey is the game's top hitter, at .377, and left fielder Adam Dunn co-owns the major league home-run lead, with 17, allowing Junior to share the spotlight. It seems he prefers this, too.

"Reporters always want to talk to Junior, no matter what," says Dunn, an off-season workout partner and one of Griffey's closest friends. "His attitude is, If our starting pitcher throws a complete game and I go 1-for-4, why talk to me? Why not talk to the winning pitcher? He's much more team-oriented than people give him credit for." Griffey has always been somewhat unnerved by his celebrity. "I'm not real comfortable with being singled out," he says. "I'm really not comfortable doing interviews in a group, in press conferences. One-on-one, I'm all right, but those press conferences at the All-Star Game, I just don't.... I feel better when I'm by myself.

"You play the game a certain way, and people think your personality off the field should be just as electrifying," Griffey says. "That's not the case." Because of his wariness Griffey sometimes appears aloof and guarded, even when he's not at the ballpark. At home with his wife, Melissa, and children Trey, 10, Taryn, 8, and Tevin, 2, he is quiet, even boring. "Barry Larkin spent the night," Griffey says of the Reds' shortstop, "and the next day he was telling people, 'Junior didn't say a word all night.'"

In response to relentless scrutiny of his physical condition and effort level, and armchair analysis of his mental readiness, Griffey has developed an attitude not unlike paranoia. "I'm the one that's got the bull's-eye on my back," he says, "and that's cool. I'm used to it. As soon as somebody says something negative about me, it snowballs [in the media]. I can't afford to let myself slip once, because if I do, I'll hear about it. With other people, it gets swept under the rug, but never with me." In conversation Griffey speaks in rambling monologues, meandering from topic to topic, but when the subject of his injury history arises, he focuses sharply on specific information: As a result of surgery to repair a dislocated right shoulder last summer, he had six screws inserted, five titanium and one biodegradable. After the operation his shoulder was so weak, he had difficulty lifting a glass of water. And his ankle, in a boot and a sling for a month after surgery mended a torn peroneal tendon, was so unsteady that he had trouble walking.

He bristles at criticism by the media or by fans because he believes that none of his injuries was preventable. "I'm in a catch-22," he says. "If I don't go after a ball, I'm lazy, I'm not giving it 100 percent. If I do dive for the ball—which I did, and blew out my shoulder—it's, Why did I play it so hard? There's no happy medium."

Even when Griffey discusses his family, an obvious source of pride, he reveals his anxiety over how his fame affects those close to him. In a youth football game last summer, Trey, a running back, was targeted by shouting fans and coaches of the opposing team. "They know who his daddy is," Griffey says, "and they kept yelling, 'Hit him, hit No. 3.'" After one play Trey and an opponent began chirping at each other, and on the ensuing snap Trey, the lead blocker, ran through the hole and delivered a helmet-to-helmet hit. "Trey just crushed this kid," Griffey says. "The kid starts crying, and they had to take him off the field. I started laughing. After Trey came off the field, I gave him a high five and told him, 'That was nice.' But the fans kept yelling. Trey's starting to understand that people are going to be jealous of who he is because of his dad."

Junior understands that from firsthand experience; he grew up in the Big Red Machine's clubhouse alongside his father, an outfielder with Cincinnati from 1973 to 1981. He professes to attach little significance to his 500th homer but allows that he treasured tying his father, at 152, on May 22, 1994, in Seattle. In Oakland for a series against the A's immediately afterward, Griffey met his father at the Mariners' hotel, found him lying on a bed, and flipped him the ball. "We started laughing," Junior smiles, "because it was a big deal. My dad wasn't a power hitter, and I didn't think I'd be a power hitter because the person I wanted to be like was him, and he was the one that taught me to play the game. I came up as a number two hitter. My first year I hit 16 homers, and I was like, Whoa, I'm rollin'!"

Ken Sr. always told his son that he would become bigger and stronger, filling out his 6'3" frame. Even now, however, Junior expresses reluctance as he situates himself among the game's elite sluggers. "I didn't think I'd become a guy who hit the ball out of the park," he says, "because I don't hit home runs like McGwire, or Bonds, or Sosa. Theirs are high, and they're long, typical home runs. Mine are little line drives that keep carrying. I've hit some that get up in the air, but I don't hit them like those guys do."

Still, Griffey lies within striking distance of that group and belongs in the same discussion as other first-ballot, Hall of Fame power hitters. Though Griffey declines to speculate on what he might have accomplished had he stayed healthy in Cincinnati, research suggests that his ailments cost him 280 hits and 70 home runs. Adding those totals to his career aggregates sketches the outline of a potential 3,000-hit, 700-home-run career, which Aaron alone has achieved.

Although a healthy, productive Griffey would seem to be a potential trade candidate (especially if the Reds, with a midlevel payroll, want to shed the five years and $66.5 million outstanding on his contract), that won't happen as long as the club remains competitive. General manager Dan O'Brien says he has neither offered Griffey to another team this season nor has another team inquired about him. How long surprising Cincinnati remains a contender is uncertain. Can Paul Wilson (7–0, 3.18 ERA) win 20 games? Can Danny Graves (major-league-leading 26 saves) save 60? By one back-of-the-envelope measure, Bill James's Pythagorean theorem, which relates run differential to winning percentage, the Reds have vastly overachieved. Cincinnati, which had outscored its opponents 264–260, should have been a .507 club, not .607, where it stood at week's end. Another stat that portends trouble: the Reds trailed their opponents badly in total bases, 871–774.

If healthy, though, Griffey seems a safe bet to continue producing. He has lost neither his bat speed nor his power stroke; after averaging a home run every 14.7 at-bats with Seattle, his ratio in Cincinnati is one every 14.2. Says Mariners DH Edgar Martinez, a teammate for 11 seasons in Seattle, "When he gets on a roll like he's back to now, he can put up a lot of numbers in a hurry. His swing and approach are just like they used to be. I've watched some of his at-bats lately, and it looks like he's back to being Junior."

Despite what often looks like petulance or distance to the outsider, despite puzzling and petty incidents like last month's teapot tempest with the Marlins—Griffey appeared to glare at Florida manager Jack McKeon in the dugout, after hitting a home run following an intentional walk to Casey—Junior insists he is content. "I'm always happy," he says. "You guys [in the media] are not in my world. People think they know me, and they have no clue. I still love the game, more than you think I do."

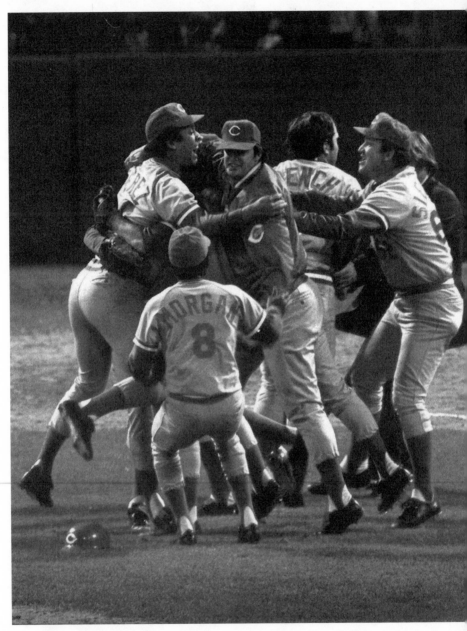

The 1975 Reds, after winning one of the greatest World Series of all time, celebrate the franchise's first championship in 35 years.

Section II
THE WORLD SERIES

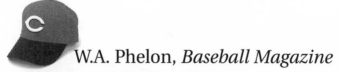

W.A. Phelon, *Baseball Magazine*

HOW THE NEW WORLD CHAMPIONSHIP WAS WON

After waiting years for a championship, imagine the consternation of the Reds and their fans alike when the Black Sox Scandal was revealed almost a year after Cincinnati's first World Series triumph. Despite numerous rumors during the 1919 fall classic, most writers and base-ball people closed their eyes to the truth, refusing to openly acknowledge the actions of the conspiring White Sox players in on the fix. W.A. Phelon wrote the following recap of the Reds victory for Baseball Magazine *long before the Black Sox Scandal broke.*

"The king has fallen—long, long live the king!" The bubble of American League supremacy has been exploded. The gabble about "the American League being 30 percent stronger" can go where Congress has put the 2.75 percent beer. In fair fight and without any luck or any breaks save those obtained by superior ball playing, the Cincinnati Reds have downed the best club of the American League, and have done it in such hollow fashion that the suspicious public even raised a howl of "Fake" when the Reds briefly slackened in their stride and the American Leaguers had a taste of victory.

There is no excuse, no alibi. The American League can't even charge it to the extension of the Series from seven games to nine. Had the old seven-game rule been in effect, the whipping would have been much worse—the series would have ended in five games, the Reds victorious 4 to 1. The stretching of the Series gave the American Leaguers a second chance—and still they were defeated. The best ballclub won, and that's the only answer.

Convincing proof that the Reds played the better ball, irrespective of all luck or breaks: the difference in the number of runs produced by the hits of each team during the Series. The Reds made 64 hits, the White Sox 59, or only five fewer safeties. Yet the Reds coined 35 runs out of their 64 hits, the White Sox only 20. That is enough to show that the

Reds played fast ball and improved their opportunities, the Sox played dumb ball and failed with their chances—or else were held, when they had men on bases, by magnificent pitching and defensive play.

It was the fiercest, most bitterly contested Series ever played, even though the American Leaguers were outclassed so badly. With the biggest money on record as the prize, the athletes forgot the ethics of the game and played no parlor ball. Never was such language exchanged between two clubs—the tide of objurgation and adjectives flowed incessantly. It was a "riding" match, and the Reds proved much the better riders. From start to finish, the reserve players of the Reds taunted and tormented the White Sox till the vaunted stars of the American League were shaking and wobbly with futile fury. Again and again, quick action by the umpires and the cooler-headed players prevented fistfights among the athletes. People who sat behind the White Sox bench say that the language Gleason's men—especially their leader—poured forth was sulphurous as the pit below, but the White Sox epithets didn't sting the Reds—half of the Chicago language was aimed at their own gang, and the Sox berated each other in hideous fashion. The Reds were just as bad, but they centered their fire on the Sox, and didn't jangle among themselves—which made quite a difference in the long run.

The pitching of the Series presented an interesting problem before the struggle even started. Could three men, Cicotte, Williams, and Kerr, who had done tremendous work all season, hold their own against five or six men, who had equally high pitching percentages, but had divided up the toil more evenly, and hadn't been strained or overtaxed? Most fans thought the nine-game Series would tell in favor of the club having the most pitchers—that the White Sox three, perfectly capable of going six or seven games, would be done up by the exertion, and would fail to keep up the pace in the two extra games, while the numerous Reds pitchers would last much better. In other words, the longer the Series went, the better for the Reds, while the Sox would have every advantage if they could dash in at the start and get a margin.

You can never tell about the dope. In this case, it worked out just the other way. The longer the Series went, the better it looked for the Sox, and the Reds would have won in a walk had the Series been limited to the original seven games. As to the pitchers themselves: Cicotte was the easiest kind of a mark in his first game. He pitched elegantly on his second time out, but lost by two personally conducted fielding errors. In his third attempt, he caught the Reds in better condition for ice water and Turkish baths than for any ballgame, and easily defeated them.

Left-handed Williams had lovely luck, not. Three times he held the Reds to a few hits and each time they bunched the few hits nicely, drove in a flock of runs, and whaled him.

Little Kerr was a real pitching hero. He shut the Reds out once with three hits, and, in another game, outlasted them and finally beat them after a grueling battle. Lots of credit to the little fellow—the man who took two triumphs from the new champions of the world!

The Sox relief pitchers were so bad that they could hardly be classified as real pitchers, and merely served to fatten the averages of the conquerors.

Moran started feeding left-handed pitching to the Sox, who certainly don't like sinister slants any too well. Ruether easily vanquished them in the first contest. In his second effort, Ruether wasn't what you'd call right to pitch anything, not even hay, and got his hurriedly, though he escaped an official defeat, leaving with the score still in his favor.

Slim Sallee, though plenty of hits were made off him, easily trimmed the Sox in his first effort, and would have blanked them but for two errors. Next time Sal climbed the hill he got a lovely licking.

Jimmy Ring showed the Sox something in the way of speed when he first tackled them—and, going in as relief agent for Ruether, lost a second bout in 10 innings.

Hod Eller made awful monkeys of Gleason's men in his first game, shutting them out with three hits and fanning nine victims. He won the final game of the Series, and was master all the way save in the eighth inning, where, aided by the glaring sun, they hit him hard.

Ray Fisher pitched a nice, workmanlike game, but was up against Kerr when that young man was a superpitcher—hence Fisher was defeated.

The Cuban Luque, going in as a relief agent, showed splendid class, and would have shortened the Series had he been given a full game to start on.

The wise men were badly upset behind the bat. Ninety-nine percent of them said that Schalk would outclass Rariden and Wingo, the Reds' pair of maskmen. Schalk caught some great ball, but so did the Reds pair, and Schalk absolutely had nothing on them—in fact, six bases were stolen against Schalk's throwing, and five against the Reds.

Gandil and Daubert both showed magnificent first-base stuff. It would be hard to find an advantage for either of them, so marvelously did they defend the initial bag.

A huge surprise was handed out at second base, where all the sagacious critics had said Eddie Collins would make a monkey of Morris Rath. Rath took care of second fully as brilliantly as Collins, though Eddie never played a faster game. Rath actually made two or three catches superior to anything done by Collins in the Series.

Weaver and Groh both made all kinds of hot stops on the far corner. Weaver seemed to have some advantage toward the last, explained by the fact that Groh played with a bad right hand—one finger so badly damaged that the little fellow could hardly hold the bat.

Risberg and Kopf performed stunning feats at short. Kopf proved the steadier, and, in the last battles, outclassed the energetic Swede.

In right field, Neale outranged John Collins and Nemo Leibold, making several catches that bested their best endeavors. Another surprise was handed out in left, where young Duncan, cool, nervy, unrattled by the Sox epithets, covered ground and handled his chances at least as well as Joe Jackson. In center, there was nothing to it. The Chicago enthusiasts said nothing could be hit over Hap Felsch's head, and that he was at least the equal of Edd Roush. Roush utterly smothered Felsch all through the Series. Roush got flies that Felsch couldn't approach, and Felsch missed the kind that Roush was eating up.

The best feature of the White Sox work was the marvelous, almost uncanny fashion in which they played for the Reds batsmen. Their fielders moved like pawns on a chessboard, shifting from spot to spot, and managing to be right where the ball was going.

With eight games played, and a lot of hitting, there was but one home run. Doubles and triples blossomed like June roses, but the only homer came in the very last game, when Joe Jackson cracked an enormous fly that fell in the right-field bleachers at Chicago.

Had the Series been played on the Polo Grounds, at either Philadelphia Park, or at Cub Park, there would have been more home runs than anybody ever imagined possible. The outfielders on both sides caught drive after drive that would have been pop four baggers over the barriers at other fields. This Series was played without artificial help from nearby stands and fences, and was therefore a good, square exhibition for the batsmen and the fielders.

The great individual plays of the Series were many and dazzling. In the first game Risberg made one incredible stop. Roush made no less than four superhuman catches, one of them almost against the rear wall of the park—a catch such as even Roush has seldom accomplished.

In the second contest, John Collins made a great capture off Sallee. Groh and Kopf made a startling stop apiece.

A catch of a low liner by Neale and a fast play at first by Daubert and Luque featured the third battle.

In the fourth game, Schalk plucked a foul out of a field box, and Weaver made two stops that fairly scintillated. Catches by Duncan, Roush, and Neale, all tremendous performances, were marked on the Reds side of the ledger.

Great catches by Felsch and Gandil, and Kerr's seizure of a murderous liner, embellished the sixth tussle. Duncan and Kopf contributed grand catches for the Reds, and Rariden snatched a foul from among the reserve players on the Reds bench.

Rath, Roush, and Kopf turned in sizzling plays in the final bout, one catch by Rath arresting a desperate Sox rally in the ninth.

Neale surprised the critics by leading the regular players of the Reds at bat. Young Duncan hit in forceful, timely fashion. Rath, Kopf, and Roush batted under their all-season form, but all of them turned in hits that counted when most needed. Groh, due largely to his injured hand, didn't hit up to form at all. Daubert, in the big Series, maintained about the same gait as during the whole season. Great help was had from Ruether and Wingo, who batted with tremendous vigor. Good old Sherwood Magee, who had waited 16 years to play with a world championship club, didn't get in at all as a fielder, but rapped .500 as a pinch-hitter.

Jackson and Weaver batted terrifically for the Sox. Schalk hit in nifty fashion. The rest of them flivvered. Eddie Collins was ridden by the Reds till he was too mad to hit effectively, judging from his average of .226. Gandil, Felsch, Risberg, and Leibold were all under their proper form, also under the spell of the Reds pitching.

Baseball Magazine

EDITORIAL COMMENT

Throughout the 1919 World Series, rumors of a "fix" and "thrown games" by White Sox players would not die, even though the conventional wisdom of the day was that fixing a World Series was impossible. Unfortunately, it was possible. Yet baseball's establishment refused to acknowledge any possible wrongdoing and tried to ignore what proved to be one of the games darkest chapters. Baseball Magazine *was one of the loudest protesters against a possible fix of the Series. This Editorial, published in the December 1919, issue of* Baseball Magazine, *sums up the publication's strong feelings on the subject.*

Triumphs rare indeed, but unexcelled are the portion of Cincinnati. Away back in the early dawn of baseball she was represented by an invincible club. Oddly enough a round half century elapses before she is again represented by an invincible club. Fifty years is a long time and yet, "Quality not quantity" murmurs the blissful Cincinnati Rooter as he turns to daydreams of what the Reds will do to the Giants and the American League pennant winner, next year.

At the close of the baseball season five years ago, John Evers was discussing the chances of the Boston Braves in the impending Series with the Athletics. A friend remarked that some enterprising plunger was offering odds of 4-1 on Connie's Team. "If you want to bet," said Evers, "grab that chance. I wouldn't offer odds of 4-1 on the Athletics against the tailenders. There are no such odds as 4-1 on a baseball Series."

Evers was right. Heavy odds on a World Series are sheer absurdity. A team good enough to win a pennant in either league is good enough to give any club on earth a battle. Besides the dope merely outlines, so far as human ingenuity can do, the apparent class of the two contending teams. But nothing is more common in baseball than to see a stronger team defeated by a weaker. The infinite uncertainty that dominates every baseball contest and every baseball series, should prevent undue confidence in either contesting club.

But that fact needs to be driven home occasionally. Hence the upset of the dope and the triumph of the Reds are good for baseball.

The scientist tells us that every plant and animal on earth has its particular enemy. The elm beetle blights our loftiest shade trees, the boll weevil lays waste vast areas of fertile cotton land, while organized baseball, in obedience to the universal law, has its own familiar pest. This pest comprises some 57 varieties of the genus Fat-Head who claim that the game is "fixed."

Cincinnati and Chicago, during the recent World Series, were the scene of much activity on the part of this addle-pated nuisance. Because Ruether blew up in the sixth game and the Reds lost out in the tenth inning, some master hand had cogged the dice. There was too much money at stake, the owners would see to it that the Reds lost, the National Commission knew which side its bread was buttered, were some of the familiar slogans of this tribe of mental pinheads.

If a man really knows so little about baseball that he believes the game is or can be fixed, he should keep his mouth shut when in the presence of intelligent people. And yet this white-souled reformer of crooked baseball is as blatant as he is ignorant.

Let us look dispassionately at the recent Series and see wherein there was any evidence of crookedness! The first three games were won because the opposing team could not hit when hits mean runs. Did all the leading sluggers deliberately quit? Can anyone imagine Joe Jackson or Eddie Collins or Roush or Groh failing to hit when a decisive game in the World Series is at stake? We doubt if even the pest would assume so much. The fourth game was lost because the White Sox could not hit Ring and because Cicotte made two errors. Did Cicotte throw his own game or did the White Sox batters when they failed to hit Ring? Either possibility is too absurd to merit any consideration whatever. The fifth game was lost because Williams was slugged in the pinches and because the White Sox couldn't find Eller at all. Who fixed this game? Williams or the White Sox batters? In the sixth game Ruether blew up after a seemingly safe lead. Was Ruether fixed? If any of these chronic croakers believe this they might speak to Ruether about it. But we would also suggest they hire an ambulance before they do so.

The plain facts were that Ruether blew up. Is this the first time a pitcher ever blew up? Moran yanked him out and put in Ring. The game went to extra innings and the Sox won out. What of it? Was it not high time they won a game?

The seventh contest Cicotte pitched and won. Was there anything crooked about that? As it was, he lost two out of three. Wasn't it time for him to win a game?

The eighth was a slugging match pure and simple. Three Sox pitchers failed to stem the tide, and there you are. Were these three Sox pitchers fixed? Fighting on their home grounds with the championship a possibility, were they likely to quit?

But why carry the investigation any farther into the depths of absurdity?

Suppose, for example, that owners were crooked enough to wish to throw a game. How would they proceed about it?

First of all they would have to take their own manager into confidence. He, in turn, would have to initiate several of his players into the conspiracy. One player could not possibly be enough, for he might not have the opportunity to play any decisive part in the loss of the game.

The only player who could conceivably throw a game would be the pitcher. But if a pitcher starts going bad the manager takes him out. He cannot avoid this even if he wished to do so, without tipping off his hand. It would, therefore, be necessary to have at least two pitchers in the plot. But if pitchers were not working properly this fact could hardly be concealed from the catcher or from the infielders. In short the only way a game could be thrown with any degree of certainty would be to have most of the players on a particular team involved as well as the manager.

Now suppose that some enterprising genius could ever get a number of star players to throw a game, an unthinkable thing in itself. How long would that plot remain secret? Obviously every player in the plot would have the owner at his mercy. A player crooked enough for such a proceeding would be crooked enough for blackmail also. The owner would have to accede to every demand from that player no matter how unreasonable, to keep his mouth shut. Furthermore, even though the players were satisfied with their share of graft, some one of them, sooner or later, would give the secret away to his friends or associates, the plot would not long be kept from the newspapermen, and then the whole would be published broadcast.

The owner would be ruined, the players would be blacklisted for all time. And for what? How much could be won by throwing a game? A few thousand dollars? Would that pay the player for losing his means of livelihood for the balance of his career and being driven in disgrace from his chosen profession? Would it pay the owner for losing a half-million-dollar franchise and being branded as a crook? Even if players were dishonest, which they are not, they have sense enough not to run such risks, risks that are practically prohibitive. A boxing match can be fixed for there are but two fighters to consider, and their managers. The possibility of fixing a baseball game is practically nil, for too many uncertain elements enter into the game and too many persons are involved in the plot.

A year ago we were listening to baseball obituaries. Some of the leading scribes were shedding crocodile tears over the game they had helped to kill, dwelling with undue length on the imperfections of the corpse.

A year has passed. The season closed has been one of the most successful baseball has ever known. And that season ended in the climax of a World Series that has never been matched.

We always thought baseball thrived on knocks, but we didn't believe it would thrive so well. The owners should pay some of these hatchet wielders for their mudslinging. Evidently their activities serve as a wholesome tonic to the game.

One idol was smashed by the recent Series, an idol reared by the biased imagination of certain writers and long sustained through the gullibility of the thoughtless public. This idol was the theory of American League superiority.

For some years the National League has been unfortunate in its World Series. At times its clubs have been outclassed by the American League pennant winner. At other times they have not been outclassed, but they have lost just the same. The point is they have lost, therefore loud huzzas for the invincible American League circuit.

Another reason for this inflated valuation of the American League has been the amazing luck of that circuit in securing the majority of baseball stars. Ty Cobb and Joe Jackson and Walter Johnson and Eddie Collins and Tris Speaker have been worth a fortune to that circuit through their personal advertising. And in more recent times the American League has secured George Sisler and Babe Ruth.

But put that handful of superstars aside and the rank and file of the two leagues has not differed materially for many years. On the whole the brand of pitching in the National League has been slightly better than that in the American League for at least two or three seasons past, not counting last year when war had run riot among the rosters. And pitching is very important. One league would excel in certain respects one year, while the balance would swing the other way the next.

And yet to what absurd lengths can personal bias go? One American League owner (in Christian charity we will not reveal his name) made the statement just before the close of the season that if the Cincinnati Reds were in the American League they would finish in the second division!

Those newspapermen who condemned the nine-game Series without the slightest basis of rhyme or reason seized eagerly upon the slim attendance at the seventh game for proof of what they wrote.

Less than 14,000 people at a World Series game, they loudly chanted, was evidence enough that the public was tired; that the interest would fall off after a certain period. Then came the eighth game attended by more than 32,000 people and away went their theories. If these newspapermen were fair they would tell the whole truth. Cincinnati, the smallest city in the National League circuit, responded nobly to the Series fever. Cincinnati turned out record crowds for three games, one of them the greatest money-getter in the history of the sport. But Cincinnati is a small city. There are not enough people in Cincinnati, or its suburbs, to furnish 30,000 crowds on successive weekdays, indefinitely. Furthermore, there was hopeless confusion in the distribution of the tickets, which kept thousands from the game. The newspapermen were aware of these facts. Why did they attempt to read from the modest attendance at that seventh game a meaning that could not properly be drawn?

The nine-game Series proved several things. It proved that popular interest does not greatly decline toward the finish under normal conditions. The eighth game at Chicago was not much under the previous attendance at that city. Had there been a ninth game and could that game have been played at Chicago, even a larger crowd would, in all probability, have been present.

The nine-game Series proved another thing. It proved that nine games is a fairer test of club ability than seven. Had the present Series gone the customary length the Reds would have won by four games to one, an obviously absurd comparison of the ability of the two clubs. The longer Series gave the White Sox a life and they won two more games before Cincinnati could annex the one needful victory. The final score of five games to three at least gave the White Sox rooters a run for their money.

Hugh Fullerton, *New York Evening World*

IS BIG LEAGUE BASEBALL BEING RUN FOR GAMBLERS, WITH PLAYERS IN THE DEAL?

One of the few reporters who sought and fought to find the truth about the gambling rumors swirling around before and after the 1919 World Series, Hugh Fullerton wrote many articles about the Series and overall corruption in baseball. He diligently pounded away as the lone crusader to uncover the truth about the hold gambling had on the game. This piece appeared in the December 15, 1919, edition of the New York Evening World.

Professional baseball has reached a crisis. The major leagues, both owners and players, are on trial. Charges of crookedness among the owners, accusations of cheating, of tampering with each other's teams, with attempting to syndicate and control baseball, are bandied about openly. Charges that gamblers have succeeded in bribing ballplayers, that games have been bought and sold, that players are in the pay of professional gamblers and that even the World Series was tampered with are made without attempt at refutation by the men who have their fortunes invested in baseball.

The National League, its own skirts tolerably clear of the mire, met and adjourned without mentioning the subject. The American League, smirched with scandal, held a meeting, wrangled, fought, and black-guarded each other and separated without an effort to clear the good name of the sport.

Some of the club owners are for a thorough and open investigation of the charges and the most drastic punishment of anyone found guilty. Some are for keeping silent and allowing it to "blow over." The time has come for straight talk. How can club owners expect writers, editors, and fans to have any faith in them or their game if they make no effort to clean up the scandal?

If one-quarter of the charges that Ruppert, Comiskey, Frazee, and Huston made against President Ban Johnson of the American League are true, Johnson should be driven forever out of baseball. If they are not true, the men making the charges should be driven out.

If any ballplayers have, in collusion with gamblers, thrown baseball games, they should be expelled instantly and barred forever from the sport.

If persons accused of tampering with ballplayers are guilty, prosecution should follow.

If Pat Moran's charges that certain persons tried to get his players drunk prior to the World Series are true, someone should be punished.

Yet the club owners met and wrangled instead of throwing all else aside until the honesty of their game was proved.

The most serious assaults on the good name of the game have been made during and since the World Series between the Reds and the White Sox. In Chicago, St. Louis, and other cities the stories have been discussed, names used, alleged facts stated until half the people believe there was something wrong with the Series. In Cincinnati, it is known that certain persons tried to get two of the best Cincinnati pitchers drunk just before the Series started. Moran knows the names of the men implicated and keeps silent.

Players Now Under Suspicion

The charges against the players are more directly injurious to the sport than those made by the magnates against each other. The public has for years had little faith and much disgust in the officials and club owners of the major league clubs. But never before have players been so freely charged with cheating.

The fault for this condition lies primarily with the owners. Their commercialism is directly responsible for the same spirit among the athletes and their failure to punish even the appearance of evil has led to the present situation, for the entire scandal could have been prevented and the future of the game made safe by drastic action in the Hal Chase case.

Chase was playing for Cincinnati. Christy Mathewson, the manager, a man whose honesty and judgment are beyond question, alleged that Chase was not playing to win in some games. He did not have proof that Chase had sold the games, but he had affidavits that Chase had told friends how to make easy money and had advised them to bet on some games. He presented this evidence to the club owners, who suspended Chase on a charge of indifferent playing. The National League investigated and found Chase innocent. He was not only restored to standing but was promoted—the New York club bought him and gave him a better job.

In the last World Series the charge was made that seven members of the Chicago White Sox team entered into a conspiracy with certain gamblers to throw the Series. I have steadfastly refused to believe this possible. Some of the men whose names are used are my friends and men I would trust anywhere, yet the story is told openly, with so much circumstantial evidence and with so many names, places, and dates, that one is bewildered.

Comiskey Knows Situation

Comiskey is believed to know the entire story: knows, perhaps, more than anyone else, and has employed detectives to watch certain players. Some of them he would kick off his team instantly but for the fight that has arisen between himself and his allies and Johnson and his cohorts. He has offered $10,000 for legal proof that his men were not trying in the Series.

Comiskey is an honest man, a baseball man who has spent his life in the game and who is known for his sportsmanship and squareness. It can be stated that he will throw some men off his club the moment he is assured that some of the teams owned by his enemies will not pick them up and use them against him. He will not openly charge that they throw games—but will fire them because they are known to have associated with gamblers.

Only the feud in the American League has kept Comiskey from forcing the investigation of the charges. He is determined that if his players are guilty he will banish them forever in disgrace and that if they are innocent their names shall be cleared.

For nearly two years I have been working to discover some evidence of what has been going on. About that time a gambler from Boston, a man I have known by sight for many years, told me that the gamblers "had men" on every important club in the country. He told me the names of several. I scoffed at him, refused to believe it, and remarked that it was not the fault of crooks like him that the game was straight.

I watched the men he named. A suspicious-minded person might have found something wrong occasionally, but, frankly, I never saw a sign of crooked work. Yet one of the men he named got into trouble with one club and there were ugly whispers about him among the players. He went to another club and the majority of the players on that team shunned him. The story was an ugly one, told by another player, about an offer to throw a game.

Last July, in Chicago, a gambler took me aside and questioned me seriously about the honesty of baseball. I told him it was straight, that he ought to know it. I know he is a gambler, bets heavily, and is in that business, but also he is a baseball crank and a real fan. He asked questions until my suspicions were aroused.

I have discovered that about that time a gambler from St. Louis, whose name I will gladly furnish the major leagues, came to the gambler, told him he had three of the Chicago White Sox on his pay roll and one man on another club, and could fix a game whenever he wanted to. He offered to let my Chicago friend in on it. The Chicagoan did not believe him. Further, being a baseball fan, he took the angle that I always have taken that ballgames cannot be fixed without that fact being discovered.

Gamblers in Many Parks

The night before the last World Series opened in Cincinnati there was something doing on every side. I have known that the business of gambling on major league baseball has grown until it is second only to horse racing, and that in Boston, Chicago, and Pittsburgh especially and in Cincinnati, St. Louis, and Detroit to a lesser degree, it is larger than on horse racing. It is the great poolroom gambling game of the country now.

Hardly had I arrived in Cincinnati when a gambler I know from Des Moines, Iowa, told me that the first two games of the Series were fixed and advised me to get wise and start betting. That angered me, and I told him what I thought of him and all his crooked tribe.

Before 9:00 that night I discovered that an attempt was being made by some persons to get two of the Cincinnati players drunk. I heard the thing talked of while I was working. An hour later I knew that some of that gang had the pitchers in tow. I am a friend of Pat Moran's and immediately tried to reach him by telephone to warn him. Moran evidently had heard of it already, as he was on the trail and rescued his man. Moran says the plot failed. The fact is that one of his men fell and did drink, and drink a lot: so much that his victory was more a matter of the breaks than his own work.

I was utterly disgusted with the thing. Before midnight I discovered that two persons were extremely active in the betting and before turning in, knew that the heavy "work" was by St. Louisans. Still I believed that they had been the victims of lying rumors.

The betting was extremely suspicious, but could be accounted for by the fact that gamblers who consider themselves wise are the biggest suckers in the world in believing scandalous stories of crookedness. Nevertheless, I took Christy Mathewson into confidence and told him what the stories were that were going around. He ridiculed them.

But through the entire Series we watched every play. Any play or move that looked suspicious I ringed for the score book. There are seven rings around plays and any one of these plays could be accounted for by the theory of accident as well as by the theory of crooked work.

Ugly World Series Rumors

Yet the story grew that the Sox were "lying down." The story spread that the players and gamblers had held a meeting at the La Salle Hotel in

Chicago and that two of the players had refused to go any further with it.

By that time the White Sox team was in a turmoil—suspicions and bad feeling had arisen. There was no further need of "fixing," if such a thing was possible. The players were so far in the air they could not have played properly anyhow.

Twenty minutes before the final game in Chicago started I was taken inside by a gambler, who told me to plunge. I was mad by that time, and demanded that he come through with some proof or shut his mouth, that he was a crook and accusing others. He laughed and remarked:

"You ought to have cleaned up on it—tipping one team and playing the other."

I was mad all the way through, but wanted to learn something, so asked:

"What do you know about today?"

"It'll be the biggest first inning you ever saw," he said.

These things, and worse, are told and even printed in the Western cities. The club owners know all about them.

If these men are guilty, they should be expelled as Patrick expelled the snakes and Hulburt expelled the baseball crooks of years ago. If they are innocent, they should be allowed to prove it, and the persons who are responsible for the charges should be driven out of the sport forever.

If the charges are true they can be proved without much trouble. The baseball authorities must go to the bottom of the entire matter of gambling.

The extent to which the evil has grown made it certain that sooner or later some player would fall. Many of the players have not avoided the appearance of evil. A number of them have associated with and even chummed with gamblers.

A great majority of ballplayers are clean, upright, honest fellows. They are entitled to be freed from the suspicion that will attach to all unless the few are driven out. The men accused are entitled to a hearing. They have had no chance to answer these charges.

The quick settlement of the American League fight, the appointment of a National League commission of men of high standing, and a thorough investigation are necessary to clear the name of the game. The owners can take their choice between that and permitting tens of thousands to believe that the sport is not on the level.

Jack Cronin, *The Cincinnati Enquirer*

REDS ARE WORLD CHAMPIONS

The Reds returned to the World Series for the first time in two decades, only to be swept by the Yankees in 1939. They won the NL pennant again in 1940, and capped the season with a thrilling seven-game Series win over the Detroit Tigers. The Cincinnati Enquirer*'s Jack Cronin covered the city's joyous celebration following the seventh-game win, and Daniel M. Daniel recapped the Series for* Baseball Magazine.

Yipee! Detroit can have its automobiles, its Joe Louis, and its Father Coughlin. Cincinnati has its world champion. And, son, you can tell your grandchildren the old town really lets down its coiffure to celebrate.

The Queen City quit bragging about the big flood and gave its full attention to a boisterous, riotous celebration for the champions of the world.

Long about 3:20, when Paul's powerful right arm silenced the last bat of the pachyderms of punch from Detroit, windows, already open in anticipation, were jammed with human forms, each well prepared to unload a terrific torrent of paper.

Frank McCormick hardly had touched first for the final out when the storm broke.

It looked like Lindbergh, just in from Paris, was coming up Walnut Street and had run into Admiral Byrd coming over Fourth Street. That intersection, center of the city's financial district, staged a celebration without equal in the city's history.

Brokerage offices, confident of victory for the Reds, prepared for the carnival before the game started. Ticker tape was made ready, telephone books were torn to shreds, waste baskets were poised, and the soft tissue of dressing rooms was added to the "snowfall."

There was a traffic jam.

This is put in the singular advisedly. There was only one jam. It extended all over town and lasted for hours. Hundreds of automobile horns were blown simultaneously in the clogged traffic. But, paradoxical as it may seem, all the drivers were smiling.

Hundreds Line Streets

Hundreds of persons lined the streets watching and enjoying the wild, hilarious celebration of the victory for which the town had waited 21 years.

Fifth Street in front of the Hotel Netherland Plaza literally was packed with excited citizenry, all waiting to stage a demonstration for the arriving heroes. The crowd began to congregate as soon as the game ended and more than an hour later they still were waiting and in high good humor.

In virtually every office building in the downtown area work stopped for the celebration. (We say this as an excuse to any boss who might have been under the impression that any work was done during the game.)

Trolly wires in the heart of town were borne down under the weight of bales of ticker tape. Enough tape was thrown out of windows to record every Stock Exchange transaction since the gay days of '29.

Daniel M. Daniel, *Baseball Magazine*

DERRINGER AND WILSON HEROES

As it did every season with the conclusion of the World Series, Baseball
Magazine *dissected the 1940 Fall Classic between the Reds and Tigers to
declare who the Series heroes were and who could shoulder the blame
for the defeat as the Series goat. Daniel M. Daniel selected the Reds' Paul
Derringer and Jimmy Wilson as Series heroes. This article appeared in
the December 1940 edition of the magazine.*

Into every life comes some pleasure, into every life leaps some woe.
And thus, every World Series has its hero and every classic begets its
goat. It is our function to designate both for the 1940 Series, in which
the Cincinnati Reds defeated the Detroit Tigers in a seventh game, by
2 to 1. As you know, it was quite a function for the good old National
League, which had lost five consecutive Series and had not triumphed
since 1934, when the St. Louis Cardinals scored over the Tigers, in a
seventh battle.

Come to think of it, that victory for the Reds climaxed the biggest
year in the history of the National League. It won the spring training
All-Star Game in Tampa, Florida. It took the regular All-Star Game in St.
Louis. And then the World Series. By the same token, it was the worst
year for the American League, which, with the collapse of the Yankees,
found itself with a 90-game pennant winner.

However, let us get to the task of picking the hero. In the aftermath
of the 1940 Series, as in the serenity of so many other postclassic discussions of the past, we are confronted with a dilemma. Two members
of the Cincinnati club stand out for the laurel wreath. One is Paul
Derringer, the big right-hander, who pitched such brilliant ball in the
final game and should have had a shutout. The one run scored by the
Tigers was unearned, and traced to a wild throw by Bill Werber.

The other candidate for the number one spot is Jimmy Wilson, 41-
year-old catcher, who came out of retirement to work in six of the
seven games; stole the only base of the Series even though he had two
charley horses; came through with a batting average of .353; and did

one of the noblest jobs of receiving, and directing pitchers, yet seen in a World Series.

Cold Fact says, "You must give the hero's designation to Derringer. True enough, he was knocked out as early as the second inning in the opening game. But—add up the stunts he did later on. In the fourth contest, he came back to tie up the Series at 2 to 2. He beat the Bengals by 5 to 2, with only five hits, and saved the Reds from being tossed out of the competition.

"In the fifth game, Buck Newsom shut out the Reds, but Bucky Walters came along and tied it up again, also with a shutout. Not since 1921, when the Yanks beat the Giants two straight with successive 3 to 0 shutouts for Carl Mays and Waite Hoyt, had a World Series produced whitewashing jobs on consecutive days of competition.

"Well, along came the seventh game. It had to be won. There was nothing behind it. No eighth game. It had to be Derringer, and he had to be good. Thirty-four years old, with only two days of rest.

"What happened? The Tigers took a one-run lead in the third inning, when Billy Sullivan singled to Frank McCormick, was sacrificed along by Newsom, lingered as Dick Bartell popped to Eddie Joost, waited while Barney McCosky walked, and darted in when Charley Gehringer's grounder was turned into a hit by Bill Werber, and the third baseman heaved the ball wild to first. Nothing very substantial, nothing earned. Even that hit by Gehringer could have been fielded."

Cold Fact continued. "Derringer, dog-tired, pitched a seven hitter that should have been a shutout, when a near shutout had to be hurled to beat a Newsom who stumbled only in the seventh inning, when Frank McCormick doubled to left, and scored on Jimmy Ripple's two-bagger off the right-field screen. Wilson sacrificed, and soon Ripple dashed in when Billy Myers drove McCosky to the center-field wall for his long fly. There is pretty much the whole case for Derringer.

"He came through when somebody had to come through, and when, very likely, nobody else on the Cincinnati staff could have turned the trick. He is the hero."

Here Sentiment stepped into the discussion. "Don't listen to Cold Fact. He makes Statistics the heart of baseball. The true ticker in the game is Romance, and I am its chief exponent. Cold Fact keeps telling you that Derringer gave five hits here and seven hits there.

"But look at Jimmy Wilson's claims. A week before the Series he pictured himself sitting on the bench, enjoying life, getting a winner's share and luxuriating through the classic. What happened? Ernie Lombardi's ankle refused to mend, and Wilson had to dig out the old chest protector and mask and go to work. Forty-one years of age. Out of condition. Bill Baker was ready, but Deacon McKechnie preferred the 41-year-old veteran to the 27-year-old rookie.

"Wilson hit .353. He stole that base. And let me tell Cold Fact something very interesting. He will insist that when Lombardi failed to appear in more than one game, the Reds suffered on attack and behind the bat.

"Well, the biggest break the Reds got came when Lombardi hurt his ankle. In place of Schnozz, the Reds got the greatest catcher for those six games. Crafty, wise, calculating, instilling marvelous confidence in his pitchers, calling the turn on the Tigers hitters in many vital spots—he, James Wilson, was the true hero.

"Every day he went from the game to an Epsom salt bath. Every day he had to be pasted together with bandages and adhesive, so he could go out and catch that game. The spirit of the Reds was this grand fellow named Wilson. The very spirit of the World Series."

Sentiment started off, but turned back. "Let me add something. Lombardi would not have hit .353. You can't pass up Wilson."

While the Writer sat weighing Derringer against Wilson, the Little Men appeared on the scene. "We want our rights," the spokesman uttered.

"You listen to Cold Fact and Sentiment, and forget that there were other players in that Series, besides Derringer and Wilson.

"How about this man Bucky Walters? He beat the Tigers in the second game, after the Reds had fallen with Derringer. Bucky beat the Bengals with three hits, 5 to 3. Remember that battle? After the 7 to 2 triumph of the Tigers in the first game, the experts saw another American League Series. Walters had to come through, and he did.

"Well, the Tigers won the third game and then Derringer won the fourth. Newsom took the fifth. Up came Walters for a second crack at the Bengals. Walters had to win. If he had lost, the Series would have been over. The Tigers had got hot against Junior Thompson in the fifth contest, but Walters cooled them off. He cooled them off thoroughly. He softened them up for Derringer in the seventh game.

"Walters gave only five hits. Four men got to second, two reached third base. He walked only two."

Sentiment came back. "Who was the catcher while Walters was doing all this? Who turned Walters into a pitcher in the first place? Who but Wilson, when Jimmy was manager of the Phillies, and Bucky was a third baseman who could not hit and whose tricky throw to first doomed him as a major leaguer?"

The Little Men became impatient. "Sentiment had his say and we kept quiet. Now let him be silent for a while. Walters shut out the Reds when a Tigers victory would have closed the Series.

"And how about Jimmy Ripple? His double won the seventh game. It scored the tying run and soon became the winning tally. Don't forget that he won the second game for Walters with his two-run homer into the right-field bleachers.

"Ripple joined the Reds from Montreal late in August. The Giants had quit on him. The Dodgers had quit on him. But he had not quit on himself. What does Sentiment say about Jimmy? And what does Cold Fact say about his hits and his catches? His catch on Sullivan in the eighth inning of the fifth game was the best fielding play of the Series. Jim dashed over to the left-field foul line at Briggs Stadium, up against the wall of the stands, seized the ball, turned a somersault, and came up with the leather held aloft. What about Ripple?

"And don't forget poor Buck Newsom. He beat the Reds in the opener. He shut them out in the fifth game. With only one day of rest, he held the Reds to a couple of runs in the seventh battle. A man is entitled to a few runs, isn't he? Don't forget that after his victory in the inaugural, Bobo got a big shock. His father died. What does Sentiment say about Newsom?"

The Writer asked Cold Fact, Sentiment, and the Little Men to close their cases and leave him alone for a while.

There was Derringer, winner of the game that had to be won.

There was Wilson, the 41-year-old catcher who turned marvel.

There was Bucky Walters, winner of the two best-pitched games of the Series. And there were Ripple and Newsom.

Not that the case was finished. How about Billy Werber, Frank Higgins, and Hank Greenberg?

First let us discuss Werber, 32-year-old third baseman who first bobbed up in the big leagues with the Yankees of 1930 and who, after bouncing around from team to team, has come to Cincinnati and has settled a Reds infield that, at times, needs his steady influence. He was all of that in the World Series, his amazingly accurate throwing to first base on one difficult play after another, his startling double play in the last inning of the vital sixth contest, and his pep, vigor, and spirited conversation at all times.

"Yes, Cold Fact, you are right. He did throw a ball badly to first base in the third inning of the final game. That error, his second in 27 chances, did lead to the run that put Newsom out in front and almost into a world championship and number-one spot as the World Series hero. But the Reds won. You know that, too, Cold Fact."

And in a series of sluggers—McCormick, Greenberg, York, Campbell, Gehringer, and Goodman—Werber finished up as the leading hitter with the noble batting average of .370, 14 hits in 27 times at bat, including four resounding two-baggers. Surely, Werber must be considered.

But so, too, should his contemporary of the far corner, Michael Frank "Pinky" Higgins, likewise closing in on 32, and also dating back to a major league debut with the Athletics of 1930. Like Werber, he was busier than a first-base umpire. Never before in a seven-game Series, as a matter of fact, has a third baseman been as active.

Higgins had 30 assists, four putouts for an all-time seven-game fielding record, better by two chances than the accomplishments of Ossie Bluege in the 1924 set when Ossie helped the Senators to defeat the Giants.

And in the fourth game, when the Tigers needed fielding more than at any time during the season, Higgins did his best in a losing cause behind inferior pitching, recording nine assists and one putout for three records on a single afternoon. Freddy Lindstrom sat in the stands and watched Higgins squash his 1924 mark of seven assists, Roger Peckinpaugh saw him tie his standard for all infielders of nine.

No third baseman since the revered Jimmy Collins, of the Boston Red Sox, star of the getaway 1903 Series, had ever handled 10 chances down the left-field-line runway.

Nor were all these plays made by Higgins of a routine variety. We can clearly recall five or six force-outs at second that were difficult and timely. On the attack Higgins also held his own with a batting average of .333, including three doubles, a triple, and the two-run homer that sent Jim Turner to the showers in the seventh inning of the third game and eliminated all hope of a Reds comeback that afternoon.

Yes, the third basemen were outstanding competitors in this World Series and deserving of some share, it would seem an equal share, of the hero's spotlight.

Greenberg went into the Series labeled the most dangerous hitter of the lot. He had won the home-run championship of the American League, with 41. He had driven in 150 runs. Hank proceeded to lead the Tigers with the bat, with .357. He had one homer, two doubles, and a triple and drove in six runs. He hit for 17 bases, the best total in the Series.

As a home-run slugger, in two parks that shrieked for the attention of a right-handed hitter who could pull into those short left fields, Hank really was a trifle disappointing. But he did better than had been expected of him. Compared with Rudy York, Hank was a triple wow.

Yes, there are claims for Werber, Higgins, and Hank, as well as the rest.

What to do? If the Writer picks Derringer, he will offend Sentiment, who is a very good friend of his.

If the Writer nominates Wilson, he will alienate Cold Fact, without whom baseball could not possibly be played, and without whom baseball writing would be too haphazard.

My Dear Reader, you already have guessed it. The Writer will straddle the fence. The hero was Derringer, and the hero was Wilson. We say straddle. As a matter of—shall we say,—Cold Fact?—the laurel really and truly must be shared by Paul and Jimmy, and we are sure neither will begrudge the other the half ownership.

The goat of the Series? Well, how about Lynwood Rowe? He was supposed to be great. He was knocked out of the second game, he was belted out of the sixth. In each affair he looked like a batting-practice pitcher.

Suppose we let the goat discussion go at that?

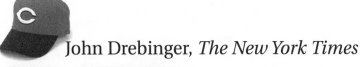

John Drebinger, *The New York Times*

THE SERIES: REDS' DEFENSE VS. YANK POWER

After a long 21-year wait, the Reds returned to the World Series in 1961. Picked to finish no higher than sixth place by virtually every baseball prognosticator, Cincinnati captured the National League flag behind the surprising pitching strength of Joey Jay, Bob Purkey, and Jim O'Toole. The trio eventually faltered in the World Series, unable to control the powerful Yankees. Before the Series started, John Drebinger penned the following piece for The New York Times *on what he thought would be the keys to victory for either team.*

This, to begin with, is not an attempt to predict the outcome of the World Series. Baseball's soothsayers know that even if the Yankees have won 18 of the last 25 in which they have appeared, nothing can be more unpredictable than a World Series.

The aim here is merely to acquaint the casual fan with what he may look for when the Yanks meet the Cincinnati Reds. It is, therefore, for this reason that in comparing the 1961 rivals on offense and defense we stress the latter. In defense, with its pitching and fielding, could lie the key to the outcome of the Series.

For on the attack it must be conceded that the Cincinnatians are scarcely a match for the power-laden Bombers. It is apparent that if Freddie Hutchinson's Reds are to win they will have to rely heavily on defense.

For let it not be overlooked that besides Roger Maris and Mickey Mantle the Yanks have four other sluggers who have hit 20 or more homers this year.

Still an Enigma

Have the Reds the pitching to check this devastating hitting? That, indeed, is a difficult question. From the beginning of the season the

Reds have been pretty much of an enigma. They were picked to finish fifth or sixth, they wound up on top in a tough league.

Who could foresee that Joey Jay would be a 21-game winner? In three full seasons with the Braves he had never won more than nine games in a year. Who could tell that 32-year-old Bob Purkey would be so effective? In 1957 the Pirates thought so little of Purkey they traded him for Don Gross, another pitcher. Don't ask what's happened to Gross. And who could foresee the extraordinary season provided by a fireballing left-hander, Jim O'Toole?

The staff may not be impressive in depth, but in the whirlwind brush of a World Series, depth is not too important.

The Pirates proved that last year. The Yanks clobbered the Bucs by overwhelming scores in three games. But the superb pitching of Vernon Law, Harvey Haddix, and the relief ace ElRoy Face, was enough.

The Reds, therefore, appear adequately equipped. For behind their three starters—O'Toole, who boasts a fast ball, curve, and slider; Jay, with a fast ball, curve, and slick changeup; and the knuckle-balling Purkey—the Reds have three fine relievers.

They are the right-handed Jim Brosnan, the left-handed Bill Henry, and Ken Johnson, a baffling knuckleballer. Also, for the middle innings, they have a young, strong, right-hander in Jim Maloney.

The Yankee Edge

Still, the Yanks seem to command a slight edge. Ralph Houk's staff not only is as well balanced, but it has the advantage of experience.

Whitey Ford, the Bombers' top money pitcher for more than a decade, is a tremendous competitor. The southpaw has been through the mill and will be entering his eighth World Series.

Though Whitey may tire in late innings, he never tires without giving ample warning. And that is where the amazing Luis Arroyo comes in. This southpaw was owned by the Reds before the Yanks bought him out of the International League last year. He is one of the great relievers of modern times.

Behind Ford are two accomplished youngsters, Bill Stafford and Ralph Terry. For the middle innings there is also Roland Sheldon, the rookie star, Bud Daley, an artful knuckleballer, and Jim Coates.

Stafford and Terry had their World Series baptisms last year. Though Terry served the home-run pitch to Bill Mazeroski that decided the Series, it never bothered him this year. And Stafford, the personification of coolness under fire, could be one of the mound stars of the Series.

Afield, the Yanks seem to have the edge. In the infield the Bombers have four top-flight performers, whereas Hutchinson has gone in for two-platooning.

Against right-handers, the Reds play Gordie Coleman at first, Don Blasingame at second, Leo Cardenas at short and Eddie Kasko at third. Against left-handers it is Dick Gernert, Elio Chacon, Kasko, and Gene Freese.

Defense Is Sharp

But no matter how Hutchinson shuffles he cannot match the Yankee inner defense of Bill Skowron, Bobby Richardson, Tony Kubek, and Cletis Boyer.

In the outfield, Frank Robinson in right and Vada Pinson in center are brilliant ball hawks. But Mantle and Maris are fine defensive performers, too.

Only in left does any one of the three Reds—Wally Post, Gus Bell, or Gerry Lynch—outshine the Yanks' Yogi Berra. But even here it must be admitted that the incomparable Yogi, the transplanted catcher, invariably makes the great plays when they have to be made.

And behind the plate, Elston Howard, backed by John Blanchard and Berra, far overshadow the two Cincinnati rookies, John Edwards and Jerry Zimmerman, or Darrell Johnson, a former Yankee third-string receiver.

Swinging to the attack we move into the domain of the Yankees. That is the way it has been since the Babe Ruth–Lou Gehrig era. During the past campaign the Bombers rolled up a total of 240 homers. The Reds hit 158. Besides Maris's 61 homers and Mantle's 54, the Yanks had four other sluggers top 20 or more—Skowron, Berra, Blanchard, and Howard. Howard wound up with a .348 batting average.

Against this all the Redlegs have to offer is the fleet-footed Pinson, a .343 hitter, and three long-ball hitters in Robinson, Coleman, and Freese. Even here the Reds lose a little, since Robinson and Freese are right-handed hitters and Yankee Stadium was never designed to give aid and comfort to right-handed sluggers.

Only in the matter of stolen bases do the Reds show to advantage, with 69 thefts, against only 29 for the Bombers. However, as the old saying goes, you've got to steal an awful lot of bases to offset one sock in the seats with a couple of base runners aboard.

Therefore, it largely boils down to pitching. If the Reds' hurlers can hold the Bombers in check they may extend the struggle to six or even seven games. But the pick here has to be the Yankees in no more than five.

Ron Fimrite, *Sports Illustrated*

EVERYTHING CAME UP REDS

Hailed as the greatest World Series of all time, the 1975 fall classic between the Reds and Red Sox also featured what is widely considered the greatest World Series game ever played, the Game 6 thriller won by Carlton Fisk's twelfth-inning home run. The Reds lost that battle but won the war the following night on Joe Morgan's game-winning hit in the ninth to end Cincinnati's 35-year drought without a World Series win. Ron Fimrite covered this classic of classics for Sports Illustrated.

A taxicab hurrying along Storrow Memorial Drive toward Boston's Logan Airport the morning after the World Series ended passed beneath a gigantic banner suspended from an overpass that was eerily illuminated in the blue dawn by a red ball of rising sun: "Wilmington Ford Congratulates the Boston Red Sox—1975 World Champions." The driver glanced up and mumbled to himself, "Nineteen seventy-six, dammit, 1976."

Later the same morning another taxi cruised across a bridge over the turbid Ohio River, which had been transformed by the sun into shimmering glass. Riverfront Stadium gleamed on the opposite bank. In the stadium parking lot the red-uniformed East Central High School band from Brookville, Indiana, was rehearsing patriotic airs, the drums thumping in the distance like heartbeats. It was a bright, joyous day in Cincinnati, and the streets were already alive with celebrants. Flakes of ticker tape, calendar pads, stationery, toilet paper floated lazily from upper-story windows of downtown buildings. These were merely preparatory offerings, for in an hour a blizzard of paper would fall from these heights on the conquerors.

By noon, townspeople had overflowed Fountain Square. Bob Braun, a local television personality, bawled into a microphone on a podium, "I'd like you to know that the lady in the blue pants suit is the mother of George Foster." The woman was acclaimed as if she had been the mother of George Washington or, at the very least, Stephen

Foster. "How many of you didn't get any sleep last night?" Braun called out. Wide-awake cheers. "Well," said Braun, "who cares?" Uncaring cheers.

Now the East Central Band, majorettes stepping out, was threading through the mob on Vine Street. "My Country, Tis of Thee," the band played and the crowd sang. Youngsters scaled trees, statues, fences, lampposts to see the parade, which was unusually short, consisting of the high school tootlers and some convertibles with empty backseats where ballplayers were expected to be.

As the Reds arrived via another route, secretaries in office buildings on the square jumped from their desks and waved from behind windows. Manager Sparky Anderson was first to pass in review, white-haired, almost regal despite his rooster's walk and down-home face. Sparky held his arms aloft and, on his arrival at the podium, bent to embrace a startled little boy, a gesture that earned him even more affection from the crowd. And there were the players: Tony Perez, the home-run hero, brandishing a smoking stogie. Joe Morgan, all in pink. Johnny Bench in a white golf cap. And finally, the idol of millions, Pete Rose, smiling and waving, an *Our Gang* character in a Buster Brown haircut. "Take it easy," Rose counseled the adoring masses. "Take it easy. We love you. You're what makes this the baseball capital of the world."

Bowie Kuhn stepped to the microphone. "I came to bring you something," he bellowed. The crowd knew what it was. "I came to bring you something this city deserves and this great team deserves. I bring you the championship of the world trophy!" Pandemonium. Orderly, Middle America pandemonium. Cheerful, Cincinnati pandemonium. But pandemonium. There had been 35 years between championships.

Anderson stood in the background, smiling crookedly as if he were surprised to be in such eminent company. The night before, facing the nation's sporting press in the interview room under the stands at Boston's Fenway Park, he had repeated a familiar boast, "We are the best team in baseball." Only this time he had introduced a modifier: "But not by much." True, save for a bloop hit and a botched double play, he might once again be standing in the shadows, not the limelight. He knew he had been lucky to escape with the trophy that had eluded him in 1970 and '72. "In all sincerity," he had said, "I don't know that there's ever been a better World Series."

He had a point, for even with the tension-dousing three-day rainstorm in Boston, few Series had been the equal of this one for sustained drama. And surely there have been few single games to match the sixth game of this Series. There have been other Series thrillers—the seventh game in 1960 with Bill Mazeroski's triumphant home run;

the fifth game in '56 with Don Larsen's perfect pitching; the fourth game in '47, won on Cookie Lavagetto's last-out double that, at the same time, broke up Floyd Bevens's no-hitter; the seventh game of the '26 Series when Grover Cleveland Alexander, old and used up, struck out young Tony Lazzeri with the bases loaded. Terrific games, all of them. But for the 35,205 wedged into misshapen Fenway and the millions who watched on television, the sixth game of the 1975 Series will be the standard by which all future thrillers must be measured.

Surprisingly, it was a warm night, 64° at game time, and the field, inundated for three days, seemed firm if not fast. The rain delay had given the Red Sox's pitching wizard, Luis Tiant, a few days of extra rest. Tiant was to have pitched the seventh game way back on Sunday, if, of course, the Series got that far. Left-hander Bill Lee was manager Darrell Johnson's original choice for the sixth game. But when the rains came, Johnson altered his strategy. There would be no seventh game, he reasoned, without a win in the sixth, and Tiant had already won the only two games the Sox had taken from the Reds. Johnson's decision did not sit well with the free-spirited Lee. In more sophisticated circles, a man of Lee's garrulity and disorderly intelligence (he is an apostle now of "Pyramid Power") might be regarded as mildly odd; in the closed society of professional sports where any intellectual deviation is treated with wonder, he is thought to be flat out balmy. Lee was, he argued, transcendentally rested, and he was also confident he could extinguish the hot Reds bats with his maddening blooper pitch—the "Leephus Ball," direct descendant of the orbital "Ephus Ball" that Rip Sewell tossed upward to batters in the 1940s. When informed that he must wait a day to try his luck, Lee remarked testily that Johnson "had been falling out of trees all year and landing on his feet."

The sixth game started well for both Tiant and Johnson. In the first inning, Fred Lynn hit a long three-run home run into the right-center-field bleachers to give the Sox early foot. But Tiant was obviously not his usual whirling, mystifying self. His paroxysmal windup seemed less confusing to the Reds, his fastball lacked snap, and his own Ephus pitches were no longer mesmerizing. The Reds were hitting him hard.

In the fifth, with one out, Tiant walked the infamous interferer, Ed Armbrister, and Rose followed with a single to center. Ken Griffey then fired a cannon shot to center field that Lynn chased almost through the wall at the 379-foot marker, his hurtling body whacking it with a thump audible in the stands behind home plate. Lynn crumpled to the warning track and remained there propped like a puppet without strings as Armbrister and Rose fled home and Griffey reached third. Lynn, everyone's Rookie of the Year, just sat there, head lolling to one side, looking not so much injured as mortally afflicted. The audience rose in stony, apprehensive silence. Then Lynn was on

his feet, miraculously recovered, a Merriwell prepared to continue—
"My back, sir? Broken in two, yes. But no matter. One must carry on."
There were lively cheers again, but they were short-lived, for Bench
slammed one off the wall and Griffey strolled home with the tying run.

The Reds broke the deadlock in the seventh when Griffey and
Morgan singled and Foster doubled them home with a drive off the
center-field fence that was so well hit not even Lynn tried to intercept
it. Cincinnati increased its advantage to 6–3 in the eighth on Cesar
Geronimo's leadoff home run down the short right-field line. This was
the blow that flattened Tiant. Johnson, who, on the evidence, had been
improvidently patient with his ace, removed him for Roger Moret, the
cadaverous Puerto Rican left-hander. Anderson, for his part, operated
a bullpen shuttle system. By the time of Tiant's tardy departure,
Anderson had used five pitchers. He would use three more.

As the Red Sox came to bat in the eighth, the game, the Series, the
season seemed at an end in Boston. But no. The indestructible Lynn,
leading off, lined a single off Pedro Borbon's leg and Rico Petrocelli followed with a walk. Anderson quickly replaced the offending Borbon
with Rawly Eastwick, who, in relief, had been given credit for two of the
Reds' three wins. Eastwick dispatched Dwight Evans on a strikeout and
Rick Burleson on a fly ball. Johnson then ordered Bernie Carbo to
pinch hit for Moret. The crowd greeted this tactic with unrestrained
enthusiasm, for Carbo had pinch hit a home run in the third game, and
if he could repeat, the night might be saved. The count on him went to
two balls and two strikes. On the next pitch he swung with all the
power and grace of a suburbanite raking leaves, fouling it off. On the
following pitch, however, he drove a ball to center that cleared the wall
and the bases and, praise be, tied the game. Carbo leaped in joy and
wonder at his own feat and danced and clapped his hands as he
rounded the bases before plunging into a hysterical mob of teammates at home plate. Johnson contrived to prolong the moment by
sending Carbo in to play left field in the ninth, the crowd celebrating
his arrival there with another standing ovation.

Carbo's heroic clout seemed a source of inspiration, for the Red
Sox loaded the bases with no one out in the ninth. Here, they fell victim
to impetuosity. Lynn popped a fly ball into short left field that Foster
caught at the foul line not far behind third base. Denny Doyle, the
potential winning run on third, unaccountably tagged up in an effort
to score, although it was obvious the ball had not been hit far enough
to accommodate such daring. Foster threw straight and true to Bench,
and Doyle was tagged out at the plate.

If Doyle had stayed put, the Sox would still have had the bases
loaded and only one out. Now they had two outs and nobody on third.
Petrocelli ended the once-promising inning by bouncing out to Rose.

What had gotten into Doyle? Third-base coach Don Zimmer protested that he had not sent him home. On the contrary, "I started yelling, 'No, no, no.' Doyle came up to me after the game and said, 'I thought you said, "Go, go, go,"'" The play represented a principal failing of our time: a breakdown in communications.

And so the teams battled into extra innings. In the eleventh Sox catcher Carlton Fisk made a fine pickup and throw of Griffey's attempted sacrifice bunt to nail Rose at second base. With Griffey on first by virtue of the fielder's choice, Morgan lined one that seemed destined for home-run country in the short portion of right field. Evans took up an apparently futile chase. At the last moment he threw his glove hand into the air and speared the ball, his momentum carrying him nearly into the seats. Somehow he regained his footing in time to throw toward first base. Carl Yastrzemski, who had moved to first after Carbo's belated entry, fielded the throw in foul territory and tossed to Burleson, who had crossed over from shortstop to cover the base. Griffey was caught flat-footed in the middle of the infield. A two-run home run had become a double play.

It was past midnight now. The game had lasted almost four hours. It was the twelfth inning and Fisk was leading off for the Red Sox. On the second pitch, a low inside sinker thrown by the eighth and last of the Reds' pitchers, Pat Darcy, Fisk took a mighty cut. The ball described a high arc toward the wall in left, curving as if to spin foul. Fisk stood several feet down the line, frantically urging the ball fair with his hands. It hit the yellow foul pole above the wall, a home run. A game-winning home run. The Red Sox had won this epic struggle 7–6. It was V-J Day at home plate when Fisk arrived, a hero of heroes in one of the finest games ever played, one that may well have attracted multitudes of new fans who had considered baseball a sedentary occupation.

"I don't think I've ever gone through a more emotional game," said Fisk, sweating from his exertions in a humid clubhouse. "I don't think anybody in the world could ask for a better game than this one. Pete Rose came up to me in the tenth and said, 'This is some kind of game, isn't it.' Pete Rose said that to *me*."

The concluding game was strangely anticlimactic, although, by ordinary standards, it, too, was a thriller. Once again the Red Sox took a 3–0 lead, achieved mainly on the third-inning wildness of Don Gullett, who walked in two runs. The Reds made up two of the three in the sixth when Perez timed a Leephus pitch perfectly and drove it completely out of the ballpark with Bench on base. Bench had gotten there because Doyle had thrown away a double-play relay, hindered at least partially by Rose's hard charge into second. Rose singled in the tying run in the seventh and with two out Morgan blooped home the winning run in the ninth on a pitch he hit off the end of his bat. In a

Series of such majesty, the climactic blow should have been more con-sequential, a wall shot or a blast over Lynn's head. But Morgan did the job. As he said afterward, "Now I can go home and say, 'We're the best.'"

And as he spoke, the thousands were already streaming toward Fountain Square to enjoy this slender, sweet victory. It is also possible that at the same time the people down at Wilmington Ford were hur-rying to edit the text of their gigantic banner. "Nineteen seventy-six, dammit, 1976."

Ron Fimrite, *Sports Illustrated*

AH, HOW GREAT IT IS

The Big Red Machine cemented its place as one of the greatest teams in baseball's storied history with their almost too easy four-game sweep of the Yankees in the 1976 World Series. "How can you have a much better team than this one?" Joe Morgan rhetorically asked, referring to the 1976 Big Red Machine. The Reds' back-to-back Series wins were the first by a National League team since the 1921–22 New York Giants. Ron Fimrite authored the article on the Reds Series sweep for Sports Illustrated.

The Reds had won the 1976 World Series only minutes earlier, vanquishing New York in the chill of an October evening as if the Yankees were no more of a challenge to their supremacy than a sandlot team from the Bronx. Sparky Anderson, the affable Cincinnati manager, smiled triumphantly before television lights that made a crown of his silver hair and stars of his damp eyes.

It was time for Anderson to explain how he had come to be such a genius. But he is a skilled practitioner of false modesty who forever downplays his contributions to his team's achievements. The Yankees did not win a game in this Series, so Sparky's strategy certainly did not get in the way; still he preferred to emphasize his occasional mistakes, to apologize for his abysmal ignorance, to construct an image of himself as the father, proud yet confused, of a gifted child. His function, as he saw it during the media confrontations that abounded at the Series, was to act as press agent for his team. After the Reds had won the third Series game by a score of 6–2, he had ventured the opinion that the Big Red Machine "might be one of the great teams of all time." Now, following the fourth win, in which the Reds buried the Yanks 7–2 with four runs in the ninth inning, he was asked if he suspected that his ambitious claim was justified.

"I wanted a chance for this club to be rated," he told the newsmen. "Now it's up to you to do that."

Actually, the rating game was already being played. It began as a rainy-day diversion when the fourth game had been postponed. Everyone from Joe DiMaggio to Joe Garagiola had been asked to compare the Reds with memorable teams of the past. Invariably, the experts backed away from the question, fearful of being dismissed as fogeys or denounced as traitors to their own generations. It was impossible, they usually protested, to compare teams of different eras.

That's true—to a point. A team should be measured by what it accomplishes in its own time. The 1976 Reds will never play the 1927 Yankees, but they sure knocked the starch out of the 1976 Yankees. Cincinnati swept New York by winning Games 3 and 4 in the House That Ruth Built—and others remodeled—and in the process the Reds embarrassed the Yanks with their daring on the bases, exposed the arms of the New York outfielders as being no more fibrous than strands of pasta, and used their belittled pitching staff to limit the Yankees to an average of two runs a game.

New York catcher Thurman Munson, whose .529 Series average was the best ever for a player on a losing team, fought the good fight, but he was upstaged by his glamorous Cincinnati counterpart, Johnny Bench, who batted .533 and drove home five runs with two homers in the climactic fourth game. Munson was further undone when Anderson extolled the incomparable virtues of his own catcher while Munson stood silently by in the press interview room under the stands. "Don't embarrass anyone by comparing him with Johnny Bench," Anderson advised the newsmen. Munson, who felt he had been unfavorably compared, was deeply embarrassed nonetheless. And so were his teammates. Confronted then with the only Yankees available to them, the Reds had turned the Series into the First Battle of Bull Run.

And that only served to heighten speculation about just how good the Reds are. Now that the A's, world champions of 1972, '73, and '74, have been destroyed by their creator, the Reds are the glamour team of baseball. And because they have the same eight players in their lineup almost every day, it is all the easier to liken them to some of the famous combinations of history.

Not that anyone is prepared to compare the Reds' motley pitching staff with such stately rotations as Jim Palmer, Mike Cuellar, Dave McNally, and Pat Dobson of the 1971 Orioles or Mike Garcia, Bob Lemon, Early Wynn, and Bob Feller of the 1954 Indians. But the Reds' pitchers, whoever they are, won their Series: the Orioles and the Indians fell flat on their reputations in theirs. That says something for Anderson's share-the-labor philosophy, which holds that the complete game is no criterion for success. His starters hold off the opposition for as long as seems reasonable, then are succeeded by the rabble out there in the bullpen. Reds pitchers completed only 33 of 162 games this season, while the '54 Indians finished 77 of 154 and the '71 Orioles lasted through 71 of 158. Nonetheless, the Reds won 102 regular-season contests and, for their most extraordinary accomplishment, seven straight postseason games—three in the playoffs and four in the Series.

After a season like that, conglomerate pitching may become the wave of the future. Indeed, if Anderson is to be commended for managerial brilliance, it should be for his manipulation of his staff. A Reds starter, unless he is a healthy Don Gullett (and there are none of those), will not grow famous under Anderson's stewardship, but he will get rich in October. Captain Hook is not all bad.

So even pitching staffs can be compared. The old Indians might serve up a Lemon; the new Reds will toss a   Billingham-Borbon-Eastwick salad. Baseball lends itself to such comparisons because it is not so much a game of inches as of decimal points. The numbers, the inevitable "stats," reveal certain truths. It is true that the conditions in which batting averages, slugging percentages, and homer and RBI totals are accumulated will not always be comparable. Not everyone plays the game on grass anymore, and the stadiums are less idiosyncratic in conformation. Styles change. There have been long-ball and dead-ball eras, periods when base stealing was considered an essential offensive weapon and when it was thought suicidal. In one of those rainy-day interviews last week DiMaggio quoted Connie Mack (now there is a parlay for you) as saying that the game changes every 15 years. The prospect of someone beating out 37 infield hits, as the Reds' Ken Griffey did this year while playing most of his games on artificial surfaces, was unthinkable when DiMaggio and his fellow Bronx Bombers were reaching base through the simple expedient of hitting the ball against or over the fence.

It is also conceded that the modern player is bigger, faster, and better conditioned than his predecessors. Logically, this should also make him better, but more than any other sport, baseball is a game of technique. A player must still swing a rounded bat at a round ball that is hurtling toward him on an erratic course. It is not easy to hit the damn thing, and extra size, speed, and conditioning do not necessarily make for a better batter. While 210-pound Danny Fortmann could no longer play guard in the National Football League, as he did 40 years ago, someone of Joe Morgan's modest proportions can still win a Most Valuable Player award in baseball.

So why not blunder willy-nilly into the time warp and venture a few comparisons? For purposes of violent argument, let us suppose that the 10 best Series-winning teams since 1920 have been the 1927 Yankees with their Murderers' Row; the 1929 Philadelphia Athletics of Jimmie Foxx, Al Simmons, Mickey Cochrane, and Lefty Grove; the 1932 Yankees of Babe Ruth, Lou Gehrig, Lefty Gomez, and a cast of thousands; the 1936 Yanks of Gehrig, Bill Dickey, and the kid, DiMaggio; the 1941 DiMaggio-led Bronx Bombers; the 1942 Cardinals of Stan Musial and

Enos Slaughter; the 1955 Dodgers of Duke Snider, Pee Wee Reese, Jackie Robinson, Roy Campanella, et al.; the 1961 Yankees of Roger Maris and Mickey Mantle; the 1970 Orioles of the Robinsons, Frank and Brooks, and all those pitchers; and the you-pick-'em 1972, '73, '74 A's of you-know-who. All were world champions and all, save the Cardinals, who won 106 games and still only finished two ahead of the Dodgers, won pennants by comfortable margins. The Orioles and A's, of course, won their divisions, then the playoffs to achieve their pennants.

Some will cavil over the '55 Dodgers, contending that they were not the best of the Brooklyn teams of the early '50s. Remember, however, that this was the only Dodgers club of that era to win the World Series. The Yankees won a record five Series in succession from 1949 through 1953 under Casey Stengel, but they were seen as if through a kaleidoscope, a succession of changing, short-lived images. It may be argued in the defense of these various Stengelian confections that many different players passed through Charlie Finley's swinging door in the A's recent world championship seasons, and so they did. But the body of the team—Reggie Jackson, Joe Rudi, Sal Bando, Gene Tenace, Bert Campaneris, and the fine pitchers—remained intact. Stengel was a genius. His teams lacked the identity the others have.

All of the top 10 shared the requisite attributes of greatness—good pitching, defense, team speed, and hitting. They had strength up the middle at catcher, shortstop, second base, and center field. Consider the Yankees team of 1936: catcher Dickey, shortstop Frank Crosetti, second baseman Tony Lazzeri, center fielder DiMaggio. Possibly more impressive were the 1941 Yanks of Dickey, Phil Rizzuto, Joe Gordon, and DiMaggio. *That* is strength up the middle.

Along with the obvious criteria, these teams possessed more subtle virtues. They could intimidate their opponents. Recall the legend of the poor Pirates of 1927, watching in chilled disbelief as the lethal denizens of Murderers' Row powered batting-practice pitches to the far reaches of Forbes Field. It is said the Pirates never regained their composure after this unsettling spectacle. They lost to the Yanks in four straight.

Few teams have been more intimidating than the Cardinals in the summer of '42. They won 43 of their last 51 games to overtake the Dodgers, then devastated the Yankees four games to one. The Series may have shifted to the Cards in the sixth and seventh innings of the third game when center fielder Terry Moore, left fielder Musial, and right fielder Slaughter robbed New York of two homers and a double with a succession of circus catches. This amazing defensive display seemed to demoralize the Yankees, causing them to believe that everything they hit would somehow be caught.

Snuffing out an opponent's firepower with such plays is one measure of greatness; taking advantage of his mistakes is another. The Yankees set the precedent for this in the fourth game of the 1941 Series. With two out in the ninth inning, two strikes on New York's Tommy Henrich, and the Dodgers leading 4–3, pitcher Hugh Casey broke off a wicked curveball (possibly a spitter) that Henrich swung at and missed for the third strike that, apparently, ended the game. But the ball bounced away from catcher Mickey Owen, and a reprieved Henrich raced safely to first. It was a fatal blunder. DiMaggio singled, Charlie Keller doubled, Dickey walked, and Gordon doubled. The Bombers had four quick runs, the game, and a 3–1 lead in the Series.

The surfacing of unsung heroes at critical moments is another characteristic of the exceptional team. Tenace had played in but 82 games and hit only five homers for the A's in 1972, but glory was thrust upon him when a leg injury scratched Jackson from the Series. Tenace responded with four homers and nine RBIs, propelling the A's past a then not-quite-as-big Red Machine.

Some teams, however, are so awesome that guile seems merely an affectation. The Yankees of the '30s and the '40s had an air of superiority about them. In a somewhat less dignified way, so did the Dodgers of the '50s. But surely no team has dominated a season the way the Yankees of 1927 did. They set records for everything from home runs to the consumption of bootleg gin. They won 110 games, lost only 44, had a cumulative batting average of .307, and outscored their opponents by almost 400 runs. Ruth hit his 60 homers and Gehrig had 47. Ruth led the league in runs (158), walks (138), strikeouts (89), and slugging percentage (an astonishing .772). Gehrig led in runs batted in (175), total bases (447), and doubles (52). Center fielder Earle Combs led in hits (231). Ruth and Gehrig were first and second in slugging, walks, and homers; Gehrig and Ruth first and second in total bases and RBIs; Combs and Gehrig first and second in hits; and Ruth, Gehrig, and Combs first, second, and third in runs. Waite Hoyt led the league's pitchers with a 22–7 record and a 2.64 ERA.

The outfield of Bob Meusel, Combs, and Ruth is still considered one of the finest defensively, and the infield of Gehrig on first, Lazzeri on second, Mark Koenig at short, and Joe Dugan on third was first rate. The team had only average catching, but the pitching staff led by Hoyt, Herb Pennock, Urban Shocker, George Pipgras, Dutch Ruether, and Wiley Moore was excellent.

The '27 Yankees have been acclaimed for many years as baseball's finest team, but there is a diminishing number of those who can testify through personal experience to its greatness. Memories grow cloudy; soon only the stats, the loyal numbers, will remain. All things are relative, though, and this team played nearly a half-century ago, before night games, artificial turf, network television, and the arctic World Series.

So where do the modern Reds stand in such august company? They are, in baseball language, competitive. They are as strong up the middle as most of the top 10. Bench regained his faltering reputation in the Series and is once again being trumpeted as the greatest catcher, the superior, some claim, of Cochrane, Dickey, Campanella, and Yogi Berra. Dave Concepcion and Morgan compare with any short-second combination, and Cesar Geronimo, with his extraordinary throwing arm and outstanding range, is the quintessential artificial turf center fielder. And though he is no DiMaggio, Mantle, or Snider at the plate, he did hit better than .300 this year.

The Reds intimidate with both power and speed. Their 210 stolen bases far surpass those of any of the top 10, though the running game was not that fashionable in the '30s, '40s, and '50s. The Reds stole seven bases in the four Series games and consistently took the extra base on Yankees outfielders. In the second game Geronimo tagged up and scored on a shallow fly ball to center, arriving well ahead of Mickey Rivers's two-bounce toss. In the same game Griffey, who has created a whole new statistical category with his infield hits, forced Yankees shortstop Fred Stanley into a bad throw on one of his typical AstroTurf hoppers. The error cost the Yankees the only game they had a real chance to win. The Reds' team speed is such that opposing infields are compelled to be wary of the stolen base. This leaves them vulnerable elsewhere, because as broadcaster Tony Kubek, the shortstop of the '61 Yankees, has observed, "With the Reds, the first baseman on the other team *always* has to hold the man on first. And the shortstop and second baseman *have* to cheat toward second in case of a steal. That opens up room for hits to get through, something the Reds take advantage of."

The Reds' panache, much of it the property of third baseman Pete Rose, is always in evidence. In the two games on the Yankee Stadium grass infield, Rose took the bunt away from the speedy but befuddled Rivers by playing in very close. In the final inning of the Series, Rivers, who must have longed to decapitate his antagonist with a line drive, finally hit one at Rose's head. Rose snatched it, then held his glove up, as if to say, "Better luck next time, sucker."

The Reds take consistent advantage of opponents' mistakes, as Stanley ruefully learned, and they stifle rallies with their alertness, as Yankee Graig Nettles discovered when Bench picked him off second base after a failed bunt attempt by Willie Randolph in the fourth inning of the final game. Rivers did manage to steal a base in Game 4—the first off Bench and the Reds in 27 consecutive postseason games dating back to 1972—but he was thrown out on his only other attempted swipe, was picked off first by pitcher Pat Zachry in Game 3, and, in his worst base-running gaffe, killed a brewing Yankees rally in the same game when he was doubled off second on a liner to first baseman Tony Perez.

The Reds also have their unsung heroes. Witness Dan Driessen in the unlikely role of designated hitter, a position the National League does not recognize except when Commissioner Bowie Kuhn obliges it to use the DH in the World Series. Driessen hit .357 against the Yankees and belted a homer in Game 3. And Will McEnaney, who endured a miserable season (2–6, 4.87 ERA), threw 4⅔ scoreless innings in relief and pitched, as he did a year ago, the final out.

People are not as easily awed today, but the Big Red Machine does leave an impression. The Reds had the best batting average in the majors (.280) and scored the most runs (857). They led their league in doubles (271), home runs (141), and steals. Five of the eight regulars—Griffey, Rose, Morgan, Geronimo, and George Foster—were .300-plus hitters. The '29 A's had six, the '27 Yankees five. The Reds have now won two straight Series, the first National League team to do so since the 1921–22 Giants.

Awesome, maybe. Praiseworthy, certainly. And during this last impressive week, praise came forth, sometimes grudgingly, from the old players who watched the Reds start yet another new era. "I'd compare the Reds favorably with any club I've seen," said Hall of Famer Ralph Kiner, now a Mets broadcaster. "The '61 Yankees don't really count. I'm not taking anything away from them, but that was an expansion year. The Reds have such balance. AstroTurf has changed the game, and they know how to play it well. They go from first to third, and if they draw the throw, they have a man on second. They're a great club.... They don't have the same power of the teams of the '50s, but they make up for it. Every man on the field is a pro."

"Concepcion has a lot more power and a better arm than I did," said the old Scooter, Rizzuto, a Yankees broadcaster. "I don't think I could play on AstroTurf so well, so deep in the hole."

"We had pitching and power," said Elston Howard, catcher on the '61 Yankees and coach on the '76 team. "They have speed. I don't think they compare to the guys we had. We had three catchers who hit over 20 home runs."

"You really can't compare eras, but this is one of the best teams I've seen," said Monte Irvin, the Giants star of the '50s who now works in the commissioner's office. "They can beat you so many ways—speed, hitting, defense. They've got a great catcher, and their pitching can't be too bad if they won 102 games. They've got a lot of guys who can pitch four or five innings and get the job done. What more do you want?"

There is one observer who is uniquely qualified to comment on changing eras. "The Reds are refined around the edges," said Waite Hoyt of the '27 Yankees, now 77 and a retired Cincinnati broadcaster. "But there was a craftsmanship, an artistic approach combined with discipline on our team." Hoyt was a Yankee. He has seen much of the Reds. Can he, of all people, compare two teams a half-century apart? There was no hesitation. "It is my firm belief that the 1927 Yankees are the best team ever."

You could look it up.

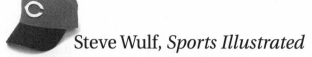

Steve Wulf, *Sports Illustrated*

THE BIG SWEEP

The Reds went wire-to-wire in 1990, spending every day of the season in first place. After topping the Pirates in the NLCS, Cincinnati bashed the defending champion Oakland A's in a surprising four straight to capture the franchise's fifth World Series crown. Sports Illustrated*'s Steve Wulf authored the following article on the Reds' sweep, which appeared in the October 29, 1990, issue.*

The delivery was remarkably fast and surprisingly easy. Quicker than you can say Tucker Thomas Browning, a new world champion was born last week, and it wasn't the team that most reasonable people expected to win, much less sweep, the 87th World Series. The Cinderella Reds beat the Oakland Athletics 2–1 in the fourth and final game last Saturday night to give Cincinnati its first Series trophy since 1976 and the rest of the baseball world something of a shock.

Stunned fans, media, and A's looked like so many bobblehead dolls, nodding and shaking their heads, as the Reds cavorted on the field of the Oakland Coliseum at 8:14 Pacific Daylight Time. The A's had won 103 games in the regular season and had breezed into their third straight fall classic by sweeping the Boston Red Sox in the American League Championship Series. The Reds had won only 91 regular-season games and had struggled to beat the Pittsburgh Pirates in the playoff. No team with so few victories had ever swept a World Series. The only other time a team had swept an opponent that had at least 12 more wins during the regular season was in 1954, when the New York Giants took four straight from the Cleveland Indians.

"The A's have the best talent in baseball," said Reds first baseman Todd Benzinger. "But we have the best team." Despite the bravado, some of the Reds were a little surprised by how easily they had won. Outfielder Billy Hatcher, whose seven consecutive hits established a Series record and whose .750 batting average (9 for 12) broke a mark for a four-game Series set by none other than Babe Ruth (.625 in 1928), said afterward, "We never let 'em get out of the box. I'll tell you something, though. I wouldn't want to be in their division next year. If we come back to the Series, I hope and pray we'll be playing the Red Sox or somebody else. I don't want to play them again. They're scary."

As disappointed as they must have been, the Athletics were gracious in defeat. Several came over to the visiting clubhouse after the game to offer their congratulations. Oakland manager Tony La Russa embraced Cincinnati manager Lou Piniella, an old friend and teammate from their Tampa American Legion Post 248 team, and said, "It was almost enjoyable to see."

The Series, short though it may have been, was memorable. It featured a newborn son, a torn father-in-law, a First Lady, a pooch, and a third baseman nicknamed after a pooch. The Reds, not the A's, played Billy Ball, their Billys being Hatcher and Bates. The A's, not the Reds, became Nasty Boys, pointing fingers at one another and bashing fellow Bash Brother Jose Canseco.

In addition to the family dramas, there was plenty of suspense, especially in Games 2 and 4. But then, as pitcher Tom Browning, who had a rather interesting week, put it, "We've had people on the seat of their pants all season."

That wasn't the only malaprop of the Series. Reds owner Marge Schott dedicated the Series to "our women and men in the Far East." (She meant the Mideast, of course, but she also might have said Midwest.) And during an off-day interview session, Hatcher told reporters, "There wasn't an empty house in the seat." As it turned out, those were about the only mistakes the Reds made all week.

The Series began on October 16 in Cincinnati, and most of the nation's baseball press brought along stone tablets on which to etch the chronicles of those Dynasty Boys, the Athletics. The citizens of Porkopolis and their beloved Reds would have none of that talk, however. At a noontime rally in Fountain Square, the emcee told a crowd of 7,000 fans, "We have to play a team that everyone says is unbeatable." After an appropriate chorus of boos, he said, "I guess you don't believe in that theory." Schott, accompanied by her St. Bernard, Schottzie, then led the crowd in the singing of "Take Me Out to the Ball Game."

As the two teams took the fields at Riverfront Stadium for Game 1, there was hardly an empty house in the seat. Before the Series, Schott suggested that her players wear their Schottzie caps (Reds hats with long, floppy dog ears) in the first inning, to which pitcher Jose Rijo said, "I wouldn't pitch like that. No way, Jose." True to his word, Rijo, a former Athletic, wore a conventional cap for his matchup with his onetime mentor, Dave Stewart.

As it turned out, the Reds could have worn nearly anything and still have won. In the very first inning, left fielder Eric Davis hit a Pat O'Brien–seeking missile near the CBS studio in left center to give Cincinnati a 2–0 lead. ("Davis Stuns Goliath" read the headline in *The Cincinnati Post* the next day.) Hatcher's double in the third, his first hit of so many, keyed a two-run rally, and his double in the fifth started a three-run rally off reliever Todd Burns. Rijo pitched seven shutout innings before turning the game over to the ever-charming, pea-throwing Nasty Boys, Rob Dibble and Randy Myers.

This was a game the A's were supposedly ordained to win, what with big-game hunter Stewart on the mound and all, yet Cincinnati came out on top, 7–0. Having knocked the Athletics' blocks off, the Reds revealed a few chips on their own shoulders. "Everybody's gonna say that this is the only game we're gonna win," said Dibble. "Everybody's gonna say the A's will come back."

Said third baseman Chris Sabo, who had a two-run single in the fifth, "People who make predictions are people who never played." When Davis was asked if the Reds had shown the nation how good they were, he replied, "The nation doesn't concern me. The nation ain't in this clubhouse." A quick look around revealed that he might have been wrong about that.

The one Red who seemed to be having a good time was Rijo. He had gotten into some hot water in the playoffs when he declared, after Cincinnati had taken a three-games-to-one lead over the Pirates, that "it's over." Asked after Game 1, "Is it over?" Rijo answered, "No, no, no, no, no, no. Yogi's right: It's not over till it's over." Then, in explaining why there's less pressure in the Series than in the playoffs, Rijo uttered his own Yogi-ism: "When you get here, you're there."

The victory gave Rijo a leg up on his father-in-law, Hall of Famer Juan Marichal, whose only World Series appearance had been four shutout innings in Game 4 of the San Francisco Giants' 1962 Series with the New York Yankees—he had to leave that game when Whitey Ford hit him on the hand with a pitch. Marichal was in Cincinnati as the analyst for Major League Baseball's Spanish-language broadcast, but he is also director of Oakland's Latin-American scouting. "I wanted Jose to pitch well, but I wanted the A's to win," said Marichal. "My daughter Rosie [Rijo's wife] doesn't understand that I have to root for the A's."

Game 2 had a family angle as well. George Bush had been the probable first-ball pitcher but had to cancel—budget crisis, you know. So Barbara Bush was named to replace him, which immediately got Schott to thinking. Why not bring Millie to play with Shottzie? Millie, the White House springer spaniel, couldn't make it, however—budget crisis, you know. So the First Lady took the field solo to throw out the first ball. Said her catcher, Cincinnati's Joe Oliver, "She had a pretty good fastball, good movement. I'm glad I had a sponge in my mitt."

After the throw, the First Lady gave Oliver a peck on the cheek, and the next thing anyone knew, she was bussing Piniella and La Russa, Schott was kissing La Russa and Piniella, and La Russa was down on his knees talking to Schottzie, who was wearing a Reds cap. One could only imagine what La Russa, an ardent animal-rights activist, was saying to the Saint Bernard ("You don't have to let yourself be humiliated like this, you know. Let me take off your collar. Now run, girl, run....") La Russa later described Schottzie this way: "She was gorgeous. The highlight was definitely getting to Schottzie. She's a great lady."

Oh yeah, the game. Cincinnati won 5–4 in the tenth inning of one of the most exciting games in World Series history. The A's finally scored a run, in the first on a Rickey rally: Henderson singled, stole second, went to third on a sacrifice, and scored on a groundout. But the Reds came right back with two runs in the bottom of the first off 27-game winner Bob Welch: Hatcher doubled in a run and scored after a fly-out and a groundout. The A's recaptured the lead in the third, chasing starter Danny Jackson with three runs, the first of which came on a solo homer by Canseco. Cincinnati closed the score to 4–3 in the fourth on a pinch single by Ron Oester that Piniella later called "the turning point of the Series."

The real turning point came in the bottom of the eighth. Even though the A's had a one-run lead and closer Dennis Eckersley was warmed up, La Russa let Welch start the inning. Hatcher—the name comes up a lot in stories about underdog teams beating the A's in the World Series (viz., Mickey Hatcher of the 1988 Los Angeles Dodgers)—led off the inning with a fly ball to right that Canseco misplayed. The resulting triple broke the Series record of six consecutive hits, held by Goose Goslin (1924) and Thurman Munson ('76). Hatcher could have scored when Davis flied to right, but for some reason he froze at third. Fortunately for him, he did tie the score when pinch-hitter Glenn Braggs grounded to short.

In the bottom of the tenth, La Russa finally called on Eckersley. He got Davis out on a grounder, and Piniella, running out of players, turned to little-used, little-sized infielder Billy Bates. Bates, who had been added to the postseason roster only because Bill Doran was injured, had a grand total of three hits in the majors. He was so expendable that the Reds offered him up in a race against a cheetah during a late-season promotion for the Cincinnati Zoo. Bates won, but the cheetah had stopped to pick up the cap that had flown off Bates's head.

Eckersley, perhaps the greatest relief pitcher of all time, got two quick strikes on Bates. He fouled off another strike. Then he swung, barely catching the top half of the ball. It took a crazy bounce to the left of the mound. Third baseman Carney Lansford couldn't handle the ball, and Bates was on first. No problem. Right-handed hitters batted .152 against the Eck this year, and the next two batters, Sabo and Oliver, hit .235 and .179, respectively, against righties.

Problem. Sabo singled to left—on a pitch Eckersley thought Sabo should have hit for a home run—to put runners on first and second with one out. Oliver bounced a ball down the third-base line that Lansford might have gotten had he been playing closer to the bag and certainly would have gotten had the game been played on grass. But the ball skittered past him, and Bates raced the cheetah home and was nearly hit by a huge white streamer that fell to the ground. Bedlam ensued.

Afterward La Russa uncharacteristically questioned the play of the right fielder, Canseco. Even more in question, though, was La Russa's strategy. If La Russa had sent Eckersley into the game to start the eighth inning, the outcome might have been entirely different. Little wonder some newspaper columnists described La Russa as "Man Asleep," a takeoff on *Men at Work*, George Will's best-selling baseball book, which includes a laudatory chapter on La Russa's managerial acumen.

The Billys could have been goats, but they were the heroes. "To tell you the truth," said Bates, "things happened so quickly, I didn't even realize this was a World Series game." Said Oester of Bates, "He's sort of like the mascot of the team."

Hatcher is such an unassuming sort that when he was told of the record he had broken, he said, "Thank you." He also said personal records didn't mean anything to him: "I want a ring. When I was with Houston, Yogi Berra used to show me all those rings, and I want one. They're pretty."

Unbeknownst to the 55,832 people in attendance, another drama was unfolding underneath the stands. Debbie Browning, the wife of Tom, went into labor during the game—her contractions were coming one batter apart—and she left her seat in the fifth inning to drive herself to the hospital. A van, however, was blocking her car, so she went into the Cincinnati clubhouse to get help. Word of her predicament was passed to her husband. Browning, who was scheduled to start Game 3, figured he wouldn't be needed, so he left to drive her to St. Elizabeth South without telling anyone. "She was in the driver's seat," said Browning later, "and I just asked her, 'Can I go?'" The Brownings, who have two other children, Tiffany, 6, and Tanner, 3, arrived at the hospital in 20 minutes.

In the meantime, Piniella was running out of pitchers and asked pitching coach Stan Williams, "Where's Browning?" Williams didn't know. Eventually, the Reds, thinking that Browning was en route to a nearby hospital, had radio broadcaster Marty Brennaman put out an APB on Browning, a bulletin that was picked up by Tim McCarver on CBS, who passed it along in the ninth inning. That's when Browning, who was watching the game in a hospital waiting room, got the message. "When I heard that, I panicked," he said. "But I decided I wouldn't leave Debbie until I knew she and the baby were all right."

He was still dressed in his uniform, of course. "I looked kind of goofy, like some sort of crazy fan who had wandered into the hospital," he said. The doctor made him get rid of his chaw, and he had taken off his hat, but there he was in his scrubs as a cesarean section was performed on Debbie. The game ended at 11:57 P.M., and Tucker Thomas

Browning came into the world at 12:37 A.M., weighing six pounds, 11 ounces. "He came out crying, 'Win! Win!'" said Tom.

By the time all parties had arrived in Oakland on Thursday, the A's were being hit over the head with all those stone tablets the writers had brought. Canseco, in particular, was hit hard. He had become the symbol of the Athletics' failure in the first two games. Even Stewart had criticized his play. To be fair, Canseco was hurt, with both a sore back and a sore forefinger on his right hand. Still, La Russa thought he should have a heart-to-heart, or toe-to-toe, talk with Canseco as the other A's worked out.

For their part, the Reds were talking about Browning, who had boarded the charter with one hour's sleep and was scheduled to pitch in 24 hours. The left-hander patiently recounted his adventures for the press time and time again as Rijo patrolled the outfield dressed in a T-shirt that read: "It's Over."

If Game 2 was one of the best games in Series history, Game 3 might have been one of the worst, at least as far as Oakland is concerned. Stewart threw out the ceremonial first ball in recognition of his Roberto Clemente Award for community involvement, but Mike Moore made the first pitch, and he had nothing. He dodged a bullet in the first, giving up three singles and no runs, but in the second he served up a solo homer to Sabo. The A's took the lead in the bottom of the inning on a two-run homer by Harold Baines, but in the top of the third, Moore allowed five more runs, two on Sabo's second homer. Mark McGwire made an error in the inning, and center fielder Dave Henderson made an egregious throw to third that enabled a runner to advance a base.

When Scott Sanderson took over for Moore, the game was over. Just to make sure, Sanderson gave up a double to Oliver, a single to Mariano Duncan, and a triple to Barry Larkin. All in all, 11 Reds came to the plate in the third, and seven of them scored. A solo homer by Rickey Handerson in the third ended the scoring at 8–3. Canseco had a chance to get the A's back into the game in the fifth when he came up with two men on and two out, but he flied out to right.

Oakland fans who left early to beat the traffic were excused. The stadium speakers played B.B. King's "The Thrill Is Gone." And for a minute, fans thought Oakland catcher Terry Steinbach was wandering around the upper deck in full armor. It turned out to be an imposter, but such was the state of things that had it really been Steinbach, the crowd would have understood.

Browning was not overwhelming, but he did give Cincinnati six innings before giving way to Dibble and Myers. Hey, he was still a little foggy from lack of sleep. "I can't tell if the last 48 hours were heaven or hell," said Browning.

He is so down-to-earth that he took "that railroad, the BART" to the Coliseum with Reds equipment manager Bernie Stowe and Stowe's son Rick. "I don't know how he's even standing on his feet," said the younger Stowe. "The phone started ringing at seven this morning."

Besides hitting what Rickey Henderson called "key home runs," Sabo also set two Series records: errorless chances in a game at third base (10) and lifeless responses to postgame questions (75). Sabo, who's known as Spuds for his resemblance to a certain beer hound, didn't seem to be enjoying himself. Said Sabo after Game 3, "I don't have much to say. I like to do my job. I get no satisfaction getting publicity. I'd rather have my teammates appreciate me."

And they do. Said right fielder Paul O'Neill, "A storybook game. He hit two home runs; he got on base; he made great defensive plays on a field he has never played on. He kind of took us on his shoulders and played the game for us."

Sabo also cautioned his teammates not to get overconfident. "Anybody here who thinks it's over, I ought to slap 'em around a bit," he said. Little wonder that Rijo was walking around with his mouth taped shut. Taking the tape off for a moment, Rijo said, "It's not over. But it's close."

Of the 17 teams that had trailed three games to none in the World Series, only three had won the fourth game, and none had won the fifth. So the odds were against the A's coming back. Still, they did have Stewart on the mound for Game 4. And what's this? La Russa surprises everybody by starting Willie McGee, who hadn't started in Games 2 or 3, in right instead of Canseco and Jamie Quirk behind the plate instead of Steinbach.

In spite of the last-minute lineup changes, or maybe because of them, the mood was hardly festive in the Coliseum last Saturday evening. One banner, its creator trying hard to get on CBS, referring to the size of a certain contract read: "Canseco Bags Series—$23 Million?" Overhead, a plane carried a streamer for Amnesty International that included a phone number and the message "Stop Torture." One of the few hopeful signs read: "It's Not Over Til Marge Sings."

Stewart sent a message—albeit inadvertently—to the Reds in the first inning, when he hit Hatcher on the left hand with a pitch. Hatcher had to leave the game an inning later and go to the hospital for X-rays, which were negative. The A's scored their only run in their half of the first. McGee hit a sinking liner to left center, and Davis dived for it. He caught the ball, but upon rolling over, he dropped it and bruised his ribs and a kidney. Davis, too, left the game after the first inning to go to the hospital, where he was to stay for five to seven days. With two out, Piniella had Rijo walk Baines with first base open. That curiously conservative ploy backfired when Lansford singled in McGee.

Rijo walked two batters in the second, but after that he was literally perfect. Mixing in what he called his best slider of the year with a fastball clocked at 90-plus mph, he set the A's down in order in the third, fourth, fifth, sixth, seventh, and eighth. Stewart worked out of jams in the third, fifth, sixth, and seventh, although he later said, "Those jams were cake."

The cake crumbled in the eighth. Or rather, the balloon popped. At the start of the inning, a yellow balloon came wandering across the infield behind the mound. Stewart walked over to the balloon and playfully spiked it. Said Dibble, "In the bullpen we knew immediately that Stewart had done a stupid thing. He had burst his own balloon."

Larkin led off with a single. Herm Winningham, who had replaced Hatcher, laid down a two-strike bunt that neither Stewart nor Quirk could field in time. When the next batter, O'Neill, laid down another bunt, Stewart picked up the ball and threw wide of first. First-base ump Randy Marsh said the throw pulled Willie Randolph off the bag, although replays showed that he was wrong and that O'Neill was out. With the bases loaded and nobody out, Braggs, who had replaced Davis, grounded into a force play at second, and Larkin scored the tying run. Then Hal Morris hit a sacrifice fly to deep right field, and suddenly the Reds were ahead 2–1.

Rijo caught Dave Henderson looking to lead off the bottom of the ninth for his 20th straight out, but with the left-handed Baines coming up, Piniella went out to the mound. Said Piniella later, "I asked him if he wanted to stay in, and he said, 'That's up to you.' When a pitcher tells me that, I know it's time."

So he summoned Myers in from the bullpen. La Russa countered with—this sounds funny—pinch-hitter Jose Canseco. Canseco grounded out to Sabo, and Lansford popped out to Benzinger. Thus ended the game, the Series, and the dynasty. "It's over big time," said Rijo.

Said Schott, "Wasn't it nice of the men to let me win one? My only regrets are that the fans in Cincinnati and Schottzie couldn't be here to celebrate with us." Then, patting her left side, she said, "I did bring something of Schottzie with me." Inside her dress, apparently, was some hair of the dog.

Though the Reds couldn't share the celebration with many fans, they did party late into Saturday night on the Coliseum field with family and friends and scores of TV crews. Drinking something out of a Gatorade container—sparkling cider, no doubt—Browning said, "I can't wait to tell Tucker that he was born while we were becoming world champions."

Browning then tilted his head back, laughed the laugh of a madman, and said, "World champions. Kind of has a nice ring to it, don't you think?"

Until the 2006 Cardinals and Tony LaRussa came along, Sparky Anderson was the only manager to lead teams in both leagues to World Series championships.

Section III
THE MANAGERS

James Isaminger, *Cincinnati Times-Star*
PAT MORAN—A FOCH OF MANAGERS

When Pat Moran arrived in Cincinnati before the 1919 season to take over the Reds' managerial reigns, pennant prospects were low. The Reds had finished third the year before, 15½ games off the pace. But Moran added a spark that was missing on the team and the Reds responded, winning 96 of 140 games to capture its first-ever National League pennant. The World Series triumph over the White Sox should have been the manager's greatest moment, but the Black Sox scandal ruined the Reds' first championship. Moran vehemently claimed that the Reds won fair and square until his untimely death in 1924. James Isaminger wrote the following obituary for the Cincinnati Times-Star.

South and North alike are mourning the death of that delightful character of baseball—Pat Moran. Human qualities they were that endeared him to everybody he came in contact with. He was outspoken, open, frank, and fair, the antithesis of sham and hypocrisy. He carried no Latin-scrolled sheepskin but in the University of Brotherly Spirit, he won his degree.

It was a privilege to count yourself as a friend of Pat Moran's. In my large circle of baseball acquaintances, my friendship with Pat was more than a conventional nod and a mechanical handshake.

I saw him as a catcher with the Boston Nationals and the Cubs and learned to know the man when he was catcher and afterward manager of the Phillies.

No man had a higher sense of honor. In his ebbing days as a player in the ranks when his baseball future was without one paltry gleam, never once did he stoop to an underhanded trick for his preferment.

Well do Stoney McLinn and I remember the trip in 1911, when we followed the Phillies around the circuit. Charles Dooin was then at the peak of his career as a major league manager. The Phillies were playing at the old home of the Cardinals in St. Louis.

In that year the press box was built on the ground directly in back of the home plate. We knew that Pat often picked the pitcher for the

112

afternoon. At least Dooin named two eligibles and Pat warmed them up, and afterward Dooin would ask him which man looked the better and Charley would select that man.

Pat Kept His Place

That afternoon Moran was warming up Alexander and Chalmers when one of us leaned over and called Pat aside:

"Whom are you going to pitch this afternoon, Pat?" he was asked.

Pat did not hesitate: "Boys, that's a question you must ask of Dooin. He's the manager of this team."

As a matter of fact, Pat knew exactly who was going to pitch, but his sense of loyalty was too strong to tell us. Moran bulked bigger with us both after this.

Here is an inside story never printed before on what happened when the Phillies decided to displace Dooin with a new manager. The owners named one of the veteran infielders for the post. The other players immediately protested. They held a meeting and sent a committee to President Baker and said they would not play under his choice for the position and that Moran was the logical man.

Baker saw they were determined, so he shelved his own selection and appointed Moran to the place. Here was an example where a manager was virtually chosen by election and it was a tribute to the esteem in which his players regarded him that such an unparalleled thing ever happened.

Pat was in the saddle in the winter prior to the opening of the season of 1915. In this playing interregnum, he made some helpful deals. He sent Sherry Magee to the Braves and Hans Lobert to the Giants. In return he received George Whitted and Oscar Dugey from the Braves and third baseman Milton Stock, pitcher Al Demaree, and catcher Jack Adams from the Giants.

Whitted, Demaree, and Stock just rounded out the Philly team and made it possible that season for Pat Moran to win the first and only pennant in Philly history.

Accident Prevented Pennant

An accident to Dave Bancroft in a pivotal series at the end of the season kept him from repeating in 1916.

He finished second again in 1917, but when 1918 dawned nearly all of his dependables were put on the market and sold to the highest bidder. In this manner he lost Alexander, Killefer, Stock, Paskert, Whitted, and one or two other dependables. The Phillies finished sixth that season, the only time Moran failed to pilot his team across the line, one-two.

At the end of the season of 1918, the baseball public of Philadelphia was shocked when it was announced that faithful Pat was unconditionally released. To this day the majority of Philadelphia fans have never forgiven the owners for their unwise, unfair action.

At the time I did not fail to review this monumental blunder in the most frank manner. I said that the release of Moran was nothing less than throwing a $100,000 asset out of the window.

No later than three weeks ago when I was preparing to leave Philadelphia for Montgomery, one of the Philly stockholders stopped me on the street. He said:

"Do you remember when you wrote that we tossed away $100,000 when we released Pat Moran?"

I remembered.

"Well, you made a big mistake."

"How's that?"

"Why we threw away $200,000. Pat's going to win another pennant for Cincinnati this year."

So that's the way Pat still was regarded in Philadelphia.

Why Pat Will Be Remembered

Pat will go down in baseball history as a Foch of managers. He towered above the average tactician. Here are some of the reasons:

1. He had the personality to win the esteem of his players. He knew his man. He knew when he had to crack a whip and he knew when he had to plait a hair.
2. No manager ever had a more profound knowledge of the fine points of baseball.
3. He knew some of the opposing teams better than their own managers. He studied the rival pitchers and hitters and helped his own hitters and pitchers through this knowledge.
4. He was uncanny in divining the intentions of the opposing force in the heat of battle.
5. He knew how to pick players and knew how to teach them after they joined him.
6. Probably no manager in America had his success in assembling and manipulating a pitching and catching staff.
7. He always had the interests of his employers in mind. He was never wasteful and would not permit one dollar to be spent unnecessarily. He never favored paying large sums for players.
8. He studied, studied, studied. When he arrived in a city to start a series, he knew just what players were hitting and what kind of pitchers they were hitting and just what players and pitchers were in a slump.

Pat Moran was a product of the Frank Selee school of baseball. He gave this little praised but true genius full credit for learning the intricacies of baseball thoroughly. Selee, who won many pennants for Boston and set the stage for Frank Chance to win his string in Chicago, was his God.

He's gone now...is that great, big rough diamond from Massachusetts, who cascaded geniality wherever he went. In the Halls of Baseball when his name is called no pinch man can step forward.

DEACON BILL MCKECHNIE

Bill McKechnie led the Reds back to the World Series for the first time in 20 years and guided the team to a world championship the following season. An expert on pitching and defense, his players appreciated his knowledge of the game. "He knew how to hold on to a one- or two-run lead better than any other manager," Johnny Vander Meer said of his manager. The Saturday Evening Post ran Joe Williams's article on McKechnie in its September 14, 1940, issue, just before the Reds clinched their second straight NL pennant.

Sunday, October 8, 1939, was an appalling day in the history of Cincinnati, along about sundown. It was like a dead city. Citizens walked about as if shell-shocked. They saw with unseeing eyes, spoke with soundless words. Streets were filled with humanity, yet empty of life.

The Ohio hadn't overflowed its banks, the vintage Pilsner and succulent Sauerbraten still beckoned the hardy gourmands. No parachutists had dropped into Avondale. To the casual observer nothing had happened. And yet a most calamitous thing had happened. The beloved Reds had blown the World Series in four straight to the New York Yankees. Only an hour or so ago the good people of the American Rhineland had witnessed, or heard via the ether, the sickening details of the final game.

They had previously steeled themselves for the worst. Few teams had ever come back to win the Series after dropping the first three games, and this was the desperate plight of the Reds. But what the good people hadn't prepared themselves for was the hilarious denouement that saw the American League entry literally run over the prostrate form of the Reds' last line of defense, namely their horse-sized catcher, Ernie Lombardi. This was something new: a catcher stretched out full length in the dust and the enemy galloping gleefully over his motionless carcass. It had the aspects of something the old Mack Sennett school might have devised. The baseball writers wrote that this comedy symbolized the relative abilities of the two leagues.

But it was no laugh to Deacon Bill McKechnie, dead-pan manager of the Reds. He had just come from the clubhouse, where he had dressed in a dull, strained atmosphere of sweaty frustration. He hadn't said much to his players. "Tough luck—see you next spring," something banal like that. He hadn't even asked big Lombardi what happened at the plate. He had simply dressed and gone out and got in a cab with Hank Gowdy and Jimmy Wilson, his two aides. Once in the cab he lit a cigarette. Then McKechnie snorted: "I don't care if they are the greatest team in baseball; we should have beat 'em and if we ever get another crack at 'em we will."

McKechnie believed every word he uttered that late Sunday afternoon. And he still believes it. The Yankees didn't beat the Reds; the Reds beat themselves. So many things went wrong in the Series, so many plays that were carefully rehearsed in practice were mishandled when situations for which they were designed came up.

McKechnie hadn't presented any alibis. He made a characteristic statement on leaving the clubhouse: "The boys did their best. They lost to a great team." McKechnie shies away from explosive discussions with the press. Only to Gowdy and Wilson had he disclosed his real feelings about the Series.

In his disappointment McKechnie may have enlarged on the lost opportunities of the Reds last October. But as the games were played, neutral observers were forced to admit the team didn't open the door every time opportunity knocked. On that Black Sunday that found the good people of Cincinnati shell-shocked, the Series, instead of being over, should have been tied. The Reds should have been even with the Yankees at two-all. What might have happened in the subsequent stages is a guess. That is, with everybody except McKechnie. "We would have beat 'em," he insists today. "We would have had more pitching left. They couldn't have used Ruffing again. He was through."

Now let's check back on the man they call the Deacon. Let's see why he's so insistent his team, shamefully outclassed in the records, should have beaten the Yanks. The Reds lost the first game, 2–1, a glittering pitching duel between Ruffing and Paul Derringer. Could the Reds have won that one? Quite easily. One of those rehearsed plays was mishandled. It was a controversial play and the wrong player got the critical hot foot for it.

The play came in the fifth inning, with the Yanks trailing by a run. One was down when Joe Gordon singled past third. Babe Dahlgren followed with a double to left field. The veteran, experienced Wally Berger was playing out there. Everybody was surprised when he threw to second in an attempt to cut down Dahlgren, instead of home to defend against a dash for the plate by Gordon. The baseball bible says always throw ahead of the runner nearest the plate. When Berger threw to Linus Frey at second, Gordon rounded third, kept on going, and scored with what was to prove the run that made the difference. A bonehead play for Mr. Berger, the press box historians duly agreed.

"Nothing of the sort," says McKechnie today. "That was one of our set plays that didn't come off right. On that play Frey is supposed to go out, take a short throw from the outfielder, watch both runners and, if a play is developing, make it at the base where it should be made. Berger made the proper play. Frey failed to cooperate. I imagine the tension, excitement, and bigness of the Series froze him to the bag. If he had gone out and Gordon had still tried to score, Frey would have had him standing up."

The Double Play That Didn't Click

The Reds played the Yankees to a standstill when they got good pitching. Their best pitcher was Derringer. He was in the box on Black Sunday. This game was lost through another fielding lapse—a mishandled double-play ball, second to short to first, the most rehearsed play in baseball.

The Yankees came into the ninth with a two-run deficit. Presently they had Charley Keller on third and Joe DiMaggio on first with none out and Bill Dickey up. McKechnie moved the infield back in anticipation of a double play. Dickey obliged with an innocuous roller to Frey, the second baseman. He made a hurried throw to Myers, the shortstop, who had come over to cover. The ball hit Myers in the chest and everybody was safe. Keller, of course, scored. The next Yankees hitter flied out. Thus the side should have been retired—the Reds should have won 4–3 and big Lombardi never would have been known scoffingly as the Sleeping Beauty.

"But those things happen," says McKechnie. "Happen every day in some game somewhere. I'm merely pointing out that if they hadn't happened to us we would have won that game, too."

To get back to poor old Lombardi for a moment, or the Schnozz as he is cheerfully known by virtue of his stylish-stout horn. What happened to him in the tenth inning of this game when the enemy started to use his quivering bosom for a door mat has remained a secret up to now. All spring in the training camp the writers tried vainly to get him to unbutton his lips. The best they could get out of him was a baleful glare and the back of his expansive neck.

What did happen to old Schnozz when all of a sudden he collapsed in groaning sections and gave an impersonation of a palooka who had just been clipped on the whiskers by a Joe Louis left hook?

"I never asked him," says McKechnie. "But just the other day Babe Pinelli, who umpired behind the plate that day, told me. Lombardi was kicked in the groin. An accidental kick by Keller, who had come in from third. One of those collision plays at the plate where the runner gives it everything he's got and the catcher must take the shock. In the crash

Lombardi came out second best. No dirty work, just one of those things that happen in a ballgame."

It doesn't take much imagination to realize how painfully Lombardi could have been hurt. After the crash old Schnozz tried heroically to stay on his feet, but the agony was so intense he had to surrender. It was here he did his Sleeping Beauty number against an obbligato of coarse off-stage sneers that grew in mockery when DiMaggio practically wrote his name and address in the prone catcher's face with his spikes to score the last Yankees run of the Series. Lombardi wasn't a dope. He was something of a hero.

So much for that. This is another year and the Reds at the writing are setting the National League pace again. Will they repeat? "We've got to repeat," McKechnie says. "We owe it to the fans and to ourselves. We've got to prove we are better than the Series records show."

Don't laugh at me, but I have a feeling this is something more than a load of gaseous flapdoodle.

The Yankees left gaping wounds in McKechnie's soul. The Deacon's vanity was bruised. This wasn't the first time the Yankees had beaten one of his teams in four straight. They did it once before, in 1928, out in St. Louis, and the repercussions were distinctly embarrassing. As a result, McKechnie was given the old heave-ho— fired after he had just put his team in the World Series, an unprecedented experience for a manager. The incident caused many raised eyebrows in baseball circles and evoked in the deluded McKechnie a determination to quit baseball for politics. And the only reason he didn't quit was that his friends back home in Wilkinsburg, Pennsylvania, didn't think he could hold down the job of tax collector. They voted him right back into baseball—and, as it ultimately turned out, into one of the most lucrative posts in the majors. Thirty thousand dollars a year would be a conservative guess on McKechnie's Cincinnati pay check.

Eight times up against the American League entry and no hits. That's McKechnie's record as a manager. Not very flattering. But it could be the record of any other manager against the same Yankees teams. They happened to rank with the greatest and most powerful of all time. (Remember, we are not talking about the 1940 Yankees.) Still, this record makes it easier to understand why the Deacon yearns for another go at the American League, and vindication.

Just to Keep the Record Straight

I don't think I am being naïve when I say he is probably more interested in vindication for the team than for himself. He'd enjoy the personal satisfaction of coming back and winning the World Series after what happened last fall—over any American League team. But McKechnie isn't self-centered. He seems to take a close, intimate interest in his players. Perhaps this is why he manages to get so much out of so little at times.

Take the Berger incident. There is no policy reason why McKechnie should be concerned about Berger now. He's no longer with the club, yet the Deacon seemed eager to get the details of the incident presented in the proper light. Berger had made the correct play. Frey, who is still with the club, had been remiss. The wrong man had been blamed. And he seemed equally eager to get the Lombardi puzzle straightened out. "If you can work something into your piece about what Pinelli told me I'd appreciate it. You can't imagine what a going-over Lombardi has taken, and without protest. A dead-game stand-up fellow."

I talked with McKechnie a day or so after he had traded Vincent DiMaggio to the Pittsburgh Pirates this year. McKechnie had been trying to bring DiMaggio in from Kansas City since July a year ago. And now he had turned him loose. Why?

"I didn't handle him right," was the frank answer. "I put him on the spot when he joined us last fall. He came up underweight, after playing some 160 games in the American Association. He was tight, eager to make good. Like a damn fool I put him in the lineup when I should have let him rest. He began to strike out, kept on striking out, the fans got on him. It was the same thing this spring. He couldn't get started. I saw a chance to make a deal, a deal that would give the youngster a fresh start and that might also help us, so I made it. He's a better ballplayer than he showed for us, but I handicapped him from the start."

The more you talk with the Deacon the more you discover he has something more than professional interest in the men around him. There was a story about Bucky Walters and how he happened to be sold to the Reds. The newspaper quoted Gerald P. Nugent, president of the Philadelphia Phillies. Nugent had agreed to the sale, so the story went, solely at the insistence of Jimmy Wilson, the Phillies' manager. The implication was that if it hadn't been for Wilson's pressure the Phillies would have spurned the Reds' unholy gold and Walters would still be performing in Philly.

"Now that just isn't so," barked McKechnie. "Wilson had nothing to do with it. Nugent was holding up players on us, players we were asking waivers on and trying to work into deals. I went to Warren Giles, our general manager, and suggested he talk with Nugent over the phone. 'Tell him if he wants to deal with us, we'll deal in a big way. We'll deal for Walters.' Giles wanted to know how much we'd have to offer. It was my thought we could get the pitcher for about $40,000. I think we closed for $45,000. Anyway, that's how the deal was made, directly with Nugent. I repeat Wilson wasn't involved in it at all. Walters hasn't a better friend in baseball than Wilson. As you know, it was Wilson who persuaded him to take up pitching—changed him from a $4,000 infielder into a $20,000 pitcher."

In the hottest days of the feverish pennant race this year, it took the Deacon a week to recover from the shock of Willard Hershberger's suicide. It is typical of the Deacon that he seemed willing to assume some of the responsibility.

"Hershberger was a moody type, a growing mental case, and how I failed to miss the symptoms I just can't tell you. I didn't recognize the condition he was in until the day before he ended his life. He missed a play on the field and when I talked with him about it, there was a strange, fierce gleam in his eyes, a look I had never seen before in a normal man. I had him up in my room that night. We talked for a couple of hours. If he had any real pressing troubles I couldn't get them out of him. When he left me he seemed thoroughly composed. I was still disturbed about him, remembering that look he had in his eyes at the game, but somehow I figured he'd snap out of it."

That he had had a mentally sick man on his squad for several years and had been in total ignorance of the fact distressed him no end. He figured he might have been able someway to bring a more comforting and healthy attitude to the catcher's mind.

McKechnie knew Hershberger as a gentlemanly, clean-living, earnest ballplayer. If anything a bit too earnest. It is difficult to find anything poetic in tragic death to talk about, but McKechnie found a gracious tribute to pay to his second-string catcher—a catcher, by the way, the critics say was competent enough to be first string on most big-league clubs.

"Ever since he was a youngster Hershberger had a love for firearms. There was something about a gun that seemed to fascinate him. The beauty of design, perhaps. His collection of revolvers was notable in a small way. He knew many collectors and spent much time in their company. When his mind collapsed, why didn't he use a gun? My thought is that guns had been his hobby for so many years, that he had developed such a close association with them that—well, to use one to end his life would be a form of desecration."

This is an angle that probably would intrigue a psychiatrist, as would the fact that young Hershberger's dad was also a suicide, by a gun.

It is much less difficult to get McKechnie to talk about his players than himself. Probably less has been written about him than any other figure in baseball. McKechnie doesn't make good copy. He's businesslike, matter-of-fact, the executive type. That's what you'd take him for off the field. He's easy to meet, sociable, unsparing in his time with interviewers. But once you get him away from the game and his players you might as well get up and leave.

On the field he becomes another person. He still moves with a certain poise and dignity, but there is a difference. Polite restraints and soft reticences are not so conspicuous. Let an umpire call one against the Reds in a tough game and you will see the Deacon walk out on the field with his hands jammed deep in his hip pockets and his jaw stuck out this far. This is when he really takes his hair down. He has been kicked out of more than one game, and there have been times when his Scottish frugality has been outraged by the necessity of paying fines for conduct unbecoming a deacon—or even a baseball manager.

McKechnie arrived at the top the hard way. He never was much of a player and it took him years to establish himself as an exceptional manager. The first was his fault, because he couldn't hit. The second was the fault of his earlier employers, two in particular. One was too impulsive, the other was a querulous, ailing old man. In both cases McKechnie took raps that weren't coming to him. Once he was fired after winning the pennant. Before that he had been fired for finishing third with a team that he had put in the World Series the year before. These things started people to asking what was wrong with McKechnie as a manager. They also started McKechnie to asking what was wrong with McKechnie. He gave himself a good mental frisking and finally decided he wasn't meant for baseball. This was when he went home and tried to sell himself as a tax collector.

Let's look back on the gentleman's career from the start. It's the story of a day laborer of the game with a wife and kids to support. Just an ordinary ballplayer, doing the best he can, hoping next year will somehow be different, finding it isn't, but still hoping.

The Deacon made all the stops. He was a sand lotter, a semipro, a busher, a fill-in major leaguer, he even played with the Federal League outlaws. In fact, he made his bow as a manager with the Newark Rebels. Oilman Harry Sinclair had the club. He had personally guaranteed McKechnie's two-year contract. This was to be the beginning of his incredible ups and downs as a manager, for before McKechnie got a chance to display his genius as a baseball strategist the league folded in the winter of 1915.

Seeing America's Ballparks

By this time he already had been in professional baseball nine years. The Pittsburgh Pirates brought him up as a third baseman from one of those leaky-roof loops—the Pennsylvania-Ohio-Maryland league—in 1907. They optimistically paid $750 for him. From then on he covered more ground than the First Lady. He was with the Pirates twice, with both New York clubs, with the Boston Nationals and the Cincinnati Reds. He never hit better than .260 in his life as a big leaguer. What kept him going was his baseball savvy, dependability, and fielding sureness. One year he played every position in the Pittsburgh infield—first, second, short, and third. This is one thing he seems to like to tell about, because he filled in for the fabulous Honus Wagner one day. "Imagine me taking Wagner's place in the lineup, and I was never good enough to carry his glove."

He never made more than $3,750 as a player. "Good field, no hit" players came cheap then—and still do. But he played under some great managers. This may be part of the answer to his own success in that capacity.

Fred Clarke, of the Pirates, was his first manager. McKechnie was impressed with his independence and self-sacrifice. "Any time there was trouble on the field Clarke took charge. It was his theory the Pirates were his team and if there was any fighting to be done he would do it for the whole team. If one of his men was beaned or spiked he'd take the matter of retaliation in his own hands. 'You fellows calm down,' he'd say. 'I'll take care of this.'" McKechnie recalls that Clarke once undressed Red Dooin at the plate with his spikes after the old Philadelphia catcher had committed an overt act against one of the Pirates. He remembers another day when Clarke kayoed Art Devlin, the Giants' third baseman, for a similar outrage. "McGraw was short of reserves at the time and he had to send Dummy Taylor, a pitcher, to third base. Taylor went, but warned McGraw in sign language that if Clarke tried to come into third again that day he would have the bag and return to the dugout." You can see something of Clarke in McKechnie today, when he walks out on the field in the middle of an umpirical crisis. He will wave his players away and take charge. It's his fight.

George Stallings, Frank Chance, and John McGraw also had the dubious delight of watching McKechnie try to knock down fences with his daisy-chain swing. It was typical of the esteem in which McKechnie was held in those days that he lasted with Stallings only long enough to get in one ballgame. He played center field, the only time he ever played the outfield in the big leagues. It was against the Giants, and that night Stallings asked waivers on him. What happened?

"Nothing happened," answers McKechnie, who is not bereft of humor. "Frank Chance knew a great ballplayer when he saw one, so he grabbed me." *Grabbed* is scarcely the word. Chance had come out of retirement to manage the old Highlanders, now the Yankees, and they were a mighty seedy lot. Anybody who could take a good picture in a baseball uniform was eligible. In this company the Deacon was known as ".158 McKechnie." Once Fred G. Lieb, the veteran baseball writer, asked Chance how he could play such a weak hitter. Chance replied: "Because he has more brains than the rest of this dumb club put together." Even so, Bill didn't tarry long.

His stay under Chance was not without certain educational values. "He taught me a lesson I'll never forget," says McKechnie. "It has to do with fining ballplayers. We were playing Washington. I was at second base and Bert Daniels was in right field. A short looping liner was hit out there. Daniels came in for the ball and I went back for it. There had been a shower and little pools of water had formed in the outfield. I heard Daniels sloshing through the water and stopped to avoid a collision. He wasn't able to reach the ball, barely missed it, and it went for a hit. Chance blamed me, said it was my play, slapped a fine on me, and shipped me to Buffalo that night. I felt bitter and sick all over. In my mind I had done the right thing. I certainly had averted a crash, and it was no cinch I ever could have got the ball."

McKechnie has fined many players, but not one for a misadventure on the field—and the provocation must have been extremely acute in the last World Series. Notably in the first game when Goodman and Craft let Keller's long fly fall between them in the ninth inning for a triple. Goodman should have caught the ball. If he had, this game would still have been tied up in spite of the earlier Berger-Frey incident.

Getting Matty a Chance

McKechnie doesn't remember exactly how he came to go with McGraw in 1916, after the Federal League blew up. He simply got a wire telling him to join the Giants in Philadelphia. He has some sort of vague notion that Oilman Sinclair had something to do with it. Sinclair was a friend of McGraw's. Like all veterans, McKechnie has solid admiration for the McGraw technique. He is superlative in his praise when he says the Little's Napoleon was "another Clarke, only more so."

Characteristically, the Deacon didn't last the year out with the Giants. In midseason he was shipped to Cincinnati along with the immortal Christy Mathewson in a deal for Buck Herzog. "I've always suspected the Reds wouldn't take Matty unless I was included," quips McKechnie. The truth is Mathewson went to Cincinnati with the understanding he was to become manager, which he did. But the great pitcher was not a success. And years later, ironically, the obscure infielder who was thrown in the deal, as parsley with a fish order, became the red-hot toast of the Rhineland.

McKechnie was hardly a riot as a Cincinnati player. When the World War came, the Deacon, not being eligible for military service, got himself a job in an Ohio industrial plant. By this time he had about decided baseball wasn't his racket. He hadn't been with the industrial plant long before he was put in charge of sales promotion, in 1919. This promised security. So he up and quit baseball for good.

"For all I know I might never have gone back to the game," says McKechnie, "if Barney Dreyfuss hadn't persuaded me to come back to the Pirates as a coach under George Gibson. It's a funny thing, after you've been in baseball a long time you miss it—you forget the headaches and heartaches."

Managerial Ups and Downs

He had no way of knowing it then, but the sun had broken through the clouds. On July 1, 1922, he had replaced Gibson as manager of the Pirates and achieved the goal he had dimly set for himself as he watched the Clarkes, Chances, and McGraws pull the strings.

The Deacon admits to being influenced by managers he played under, yet no critic has ever written that he plays "Clarke baseball," "McGraw baseball," and so forth. On the contrary, they dismiss him as a book manager. This suggests he follows the classic elementals of the game in all his maneuvers, plays it out of the book, strings along with the percentages, eschews chance.

I asked McKechnie about this. "A book manager? Well, what does that mean? If it means taking advantage of obvious opportunities, pulling your infield in for a play at the plate, moving it back for a double play, waiting out wild or tiring pitchers, bunting on poor-fielding pitchers, running on catchers who can't throw, sending men home on weak-armed outfielders; if that's what it means, I plead guilty. I am a book manager. Show me a manager who isn't and I'll show you a manager who loses a lot of games he ought to win."

Up to now McKechnie has won championships in three different cities, which is something of a record. He won with the Pirates in 1925, the Cardinals in 1928, and the Reds in 1939. Only with the Pirates was he able to come out on top in the World Series. This was a masterful job that has not received the attention it merits. McKechnie brought the Pirates back to winning form after they had dropped three of the first four games and apparently were in full retreat. There isn't anything in the book that will help a manager in a spot like this. Only an inspirational force can accomplish this, and book managers aren't supposed to be inspired at any time. McKechnie drove his Pirates to snatch victory from defeat in one of those minor miracles of the sports pages. The Deacon must have had something besides a book of figures and a plug of tobacco in his hip pocket.

Next season the Pirates finished third in a typical National League dipsy-doole scramble. This was a disappointment to Dreyfuss, the owner, by now a sickly, impatient old man. He called McKechnie in and gave him his hat. It hadn't been the Deacon's understanding a manager must win every year. He was surprised and shocked. But as it developed he hadn't seen anything yet. Two years later Sam Breadon was to toss him out on his ear for winning the pennant in St. Louis. Not just missing it, but for winning it. No wonder the fans asked: What's wrong with a fellow who can't keep a job even when he wins pennants?

There was nothing wrong with him. Old man Dreyfuss had lost his touch. As for Breadon, an impulsive Irisher from New York's turbulent

West Side, and a good sport by any reckoning, he made a mistake. He publicly admitted as much later.

McKechnie was back in the minors, managing Rochester, the year after he had won the pennant in St. Louis. He was angry and bewildered, but he had a wife and four kids to support and baseball was all he knew. Anyway, in the fall he would go after that tax collector's job in Wilkinsburg.

One night the phone rang. Warren Giles, then head of the Rochester club and now general manager of the Cincinnati club, answered it.

"You want what?" cried Giles. "You just fired him!"

It was Sam Breadon. He wanted Giles to send McKechnie back to manage the Cardinals.

"I know I fired him, but I made an awful mistake. Send him back."

McKechnie was reluctant. He had Rochester far out in front in the International League race, and for the second time in his baseball career he had made up his mind to quit the game. But in the end he weakened. Breadon arranged a welcoming dinner for him at one of the country clubs. All the brass hats of the Missouri metropolis were there. Breadon made an extraordinary speech for a club owner: "I want you all to know I was dead wrong in letting McKechnie go. I pulled a prize boner. He's the best manager in baseball. And if any of you want to come over here and give me a good swift kick, I'll take it."

Breadon wanted McKechnie to sign a two-year contract, but in the meantime one Judge Emil Fuchs, who had taken over the Boston Nationals, came forward with a four-year contract at more money. "You'd better take it, Bill," advised Breadon. "That's better than I can do for you."

Well, Eight Years in One Place!

McKechnie didn't take it right away. He waited until those votes were counted in Wilkinsburg. It didn't take long to count them, not the McKechnie votes, anyway, and in due time the frustrated politician found himself in Boston.

He didn't win any pennants in Boston, but the manner in which he handled mediocre players stamped him as an unusually competent manager. He attracted more national attention with losing Boston teams than he ever did with pennant-winning teams in Pittsburgh and St. Louis. He stayed in Boston eight years, put the club in the first division twice, and was Babe Ruth's last manager, nominally at least.

This was in 1935, when the Babe switched over to the National League. The club's finances were shaky and Fuchs had brought Ruth in as a box-office stimulant, spraying the big fellow liberally with the old oil. He gave him more titles than the exalted ruler of a colored lodge. Assistant vice president, assistant manager, assistant right fielder.

Babe wanted to become a big-league manager. This looked like the chance he had been looking for. He had quit the Yankees the fall before when that job was denied him. Fuchs never had any intention of making him manager of the Braves, but the fans interpreted the move that way.

The situation was unpleasant and embarrassing for the Deacon. Fuchs hadn't told McKechnie a word about bringing Ruth in. The first news he got came from baseball writers. "Great for the club. Babe ought to help us a lot," commented McKechnie, pretending he had been consulted by Fuchs.

Babe had his own way, of course, just as he always had with the Yankees. Presently Ruth sensed that he was being used as a commercial come-on, that Fuchs had no thought of putting him in charge of the team. He quit in June, disgusted. He didn't reveal his decision to any of the club officials. He called the Boston writers into the clubhouse before the game and told them briefly but emphatically he was "getting the hell out of this dump."

McKechnie and the other players were squirming into their monkey suits at the time. There was a period of painful silence. Finally, one of the players reached in his locker, drew out a baseball, and took it over to the Babe. "Sign this for me, will you, Babe? I want to take it home and keep it." One by one, all the players took balls to the Babe for his signature. These weren't bug-eyed fans, they were hardened ballplayers, yet they wanted something to show they had played on the same team with the great man. McKechnie says it was the most impressive manifestation of honest admiration he ever saw.

By now other clubs began to angle for McKechnie's services. In the fall of 1938 he had a choice of four big-league jobs. He chose Cincinnati. Warren Giles was out there running the business office and this guaranteed a pleasant association. But as always there was an agitated insect in the ointment. The good people of Cincinnati had already picked the manager. It was to be Kiki Cuyler, the veteran outfielder.

Powel Crosley, the radio magnate, may own the Reds. But the natives are very fair-minded, all they ask is permission to run them. The city was flooded with We-Want-Cuyler petitions. When you boarded a streetcar the conductor handed you a petition to sign before he asked for your fare. A committee called on Giles. It had to be explained most delicately that McKechnie had already been signed.

"You just wait and see," purred the cornered Giles. "This fellow's the best manager in baseball. He'll bring us a championship in two years at least. Maybe even this year." The Cuylerites capitulated but warned, "He'd better be good."

The Deacon, who had taken over an eighth-place club, came close to winning the flag his first year. Might have, if left-handed Leo

Grissom hadn't tried to steal second base in a late-season game. Grissom snapped a bone in his ankle in the senseless attempt, and was through for the year. The Reds finished only six games out of first place. Grissom's presence might have made the difference. Last year the Deacon definitely made Prophet Giles look good. But here and there a sour note sounded. It wasn't McKechnie's team that won, it was Larry MacPhail's. Just look and see. MacPhail had brought all those players in before he left to take charge of the Brooklyn front office. "Sure, McKechnie's all right, but give credit where credit is due, I always say...."

"What difference does it make as long as we win?" says McKechnie, looking out at you over his glasses, a significant twinkle in his eyes. "Certainly some of the men MacPhail brought in helped the club. Personally I wish he had brought more in."

Was it MacPhail's club or McKechnie's? The facts are these: MacPhail is responsible for pitchers Vander Meer and Thompson, infielders McCormick and Myers, outfielders Goodman and Craft. But Lombardi was there before MacPhail, and so was Derringer. Also, after MacPhail came pitcher Walters, catcher Hershberger, and infielders Frey and Werber. Two players were mainly responsible for the Reds' championship last season: Walters and Derringer. McKechnie brought one of them in, the other was there when he arrived, and before MacPhail. If it is true that MacPhail started the Reds on the upswing, which he did, then it is just as true that the Deacon put on the finishing touches.

They call him the Deacon because he sang in the Methodist choir, back home, for 20 years. Sang until his voice wore out. "And don't write that I wore it out yelling at umpires either."

Murray Olderman, *The Sporting News*

REDS WIPE THAT SCOWL OFF HUTCH'S FACE

One of the saddest days in the history of the Cincinnati Reds was when Fred Hutchinson had to step away from his managerial duties in August 1964 because of cancer. The Reds made a late rush for the pennant and tried desperately to win to the flag for their fallen manager, but they came up just short. Hutchinson passed away less than three months later, on November 12. Murray Olderman's article for The Sporting News *reflects on happier times for Hutch and the Reds—the 1961 pennant-winning season. It appeared in the magazine on August 2, 1961.*

Fred Hutchinson, a guy once said, always looks like he just lost an argument with an umpire.

Now we've seen an impish simple smile break down those ridges of granite hewed into an immobility that has occasionally prompted people to call Hutch "Stone Face."

Especially as the years have worked on those long lines and furrows that somehow resemble a basset hound with his perpetually worried look.

The basset isn't quite as solemn as he appears, and neither is Hutch. As the manager of the Cincinnati Reds, he's got good reason to let the light lines crinkle around the corners of his eyes and a flicker of satisfaction play around his lips. He worked hard last spring to whip a downgraded collection of players into a cohesive unit, and the results showed in a six-game lead.

A slump chipped off five games shortly thereafter, but they shook it off when they beat the Giants in a doubleheader, July 23. They won the next game, against Milwaukee, 9 to 3, July 24, before being stopped by Lew Burdette, who blanked them, 2 to 0, July 25.

Fred has even become pacificistic toward umps, dugout fixtures, and lightbulbs. The Hutch one sees in a contemplative crouch on the steps of the dugout at Crosley Field used to undergo a schizophrenic change when he thought the men in blue or his own pinstriped Reds blew one.

Expert at Busting Furniture

He was capable of letting loose a stream of articulate vehemence in red-necked language while his jugular vein danced on the side of his neck in a crimson rage. If that didn't satisfy, he might splinter furniture. And he still holds the record for smashing lightbulbs in the runway at Briggs Stadium in Detroit.

The memories bring a smile of embarrassment to the Reds' pilot.

"As you get older," he shrugs, "you get mellow."

It's hard to believe the big guy is rounding out a decade of managing because he's only now on the verge of 42 and shows the same rugged physique, strongly set on his 6'2" frame, that he had as a kid of 20 first reporting to the majors in '38.

Also unchanged is the driving determination that made him, without the snap of a fastball and only a wrinkle of a curve, the winner of 95 games as a pitcher for the Tigers, jammed mostly into six big seasons from 1946 through 1951.

Top Competitor on Mound

"Hutch," said his mound aid, Jim Turner, "was my kind of pitcher—a vicious competitor on the mound, with the aggressiveness you have to admire."

"We've been playing good," conceded Hutchinson as he sat in his manager's office at Crosley Field.

"We have momentum, great desire...and ability."

It sounded like a team he was proud of and yet just this past spring disgusted after an exhibition game, he read the riot act and termed their performance the worst he had ever seen on a baseball field.

There is a tendency to disparage the ability of the Reds to stick it out through the schedule as the pacesetter, to deny them the class of champions.

"We're a young team," nodded Hutch. "I can see their point of view. But that doesn't mean I buy it. We snapped back well."

Shrewd Handler of Men

Hutchinson is chary in his judgments, so it's interesting to see the way he's handled the individual components of a team that finished sixth last season, 28 games off the pace, how he has buoyed some of the old timers, sat on the kids.

For instance, he's gone on record as declaring Gerry Lynch is "the best pinch-hitter I've ever seen." For years, Lynch has moaned about not being used every day, about his desire to be traded to a club where he could be an outfield regular. But as long as Hutch has him earmarked for something special—it's never demeaning to be best in anything—Lynch has been giving the club the kind of clutch hitting Dusty Rhodes once provided the New York Giants on a title binge, in 1954.

His outfield morale could be further complicated by the presence of two other veterans, Gus Bell and Wally Post, with highly successful backgrounds but only one job available. Hutch has platooned them, made sure neither got rusty, and has been getting valuable service from both of them.

The big men, of course, are Frank Robinson and Vada Pinson.

Ignored Robinson Incident

Another manager might have worried about the effect on Robinson of an off-season escapade in which he was charged with the possession of a concealed weapon. To Hutchinson, it simply doesn't exist. Robinson is his take-charge player, a man right up at the top of the league in his ability to carry a club.

Pinson, everybody knows, is going to be the new Willie Mays. Hutchinson soft-pedals it. "Give him time," he said. "He's a kid. Only 22. He still makes mistakes. In a couple or three years, he'll be a fine player."

His pitching ace is Joey Jay, who was picking up fat a year ago on the Milwaukee bench. The first thing Hutchinson told Jay this spring was that he'd get a chance to pitch. Jay's first reaction was wariness. He'd heard that one before, with the Braves. He didn't know Hutch.

Lets Turner Handle Hurlers

"That's all I did for him," reiterated Hutchinson. "Let him pitch. Oh, I told him not to try to outcute anybody. But when it comes to actually working with the pitchers, I have a good coach in Turner. He's done a fine job.

"I think the pitching has been the predominant figure for us this season. That, and getting Blasingame to play second. Don has knitted the infield. I had him in St. Louis, and I knew what he could do."

For three years, Eddie Kasko was regarded as a fill-in infielder, with the Cards and Reds. He could play second, short, and third and not hurt you. Hutch made him an everyday performer last year, mostly at third, and he was named the Most Valuable Red by the Cincinnati chapter of the Baseball Writers' Association.

Roy McMillan, perennially the finest shortstop in the National League, was traded to Milwaukee. Kasko became the regular shortstop. To Hutch, it was simple: "I knew he was a good ballplayer."

That's about as revealing as the Cincinnati manager gets. A session with Hutch isn't played for laughs, as it might have been with Casey Stengel or it might be today with Jimmie Dykes. He's the prototype of a strong, silent breed that is coming into managerial prominence. Walter Alston, Ralph Houk, Al Dark, Mickey Vernon, Johnny Keane— they are all players' managers, like Hutch.

There is a façade of simplicity in the way Hutch wards off pryers, ducks comparisons, shies from controversies and sometimes resorts to a welter of platitudes. Yet behind it is a complex man, a brooder, and one not afraid to exercise judgment and experiment with innovation.

The respect for his ability was apparent when he was named American League player representative. Then he was on the active rolls of the Tigers and lugged a typewriter around the circuit to keep up his homework. The question of maturity was never brought up when Hutch replaced Red Rolfe as the manager of the Tigers on July 5, 1952. He was 32 and it was his first experience at handling a club.

The future of a manager, like a football coach, is only to get fired, and so Hutch has had his ups and downs through his two and one-half years with the Tigers, three in St. Louis (he was the National League Manager of the Year for bringing the Cards up to second place in 1957), and now is in his third year at Cincy.

These hitches were broken up by a couple of stretches in Seattle, the old hometown where Fred made his initial impact on baseball as a kid right out of high school, winning 25 games in Triple A ball (he never played or managed lower than that).

When he went back to Seattle in 1959, after the dismay of his departure from St. Louis, Hutch's contract also embraced front-office duties.

He never sank his teeth into the paperwork because Cincinnati yanked him back to the majors in July, but he did get something out of the front-office experience.

"I learned enough about it," said the Reds skipper, "not to want to get to do it again, ever."

And he grinned.

Jim Schottelkotte, *The Cincinnati Enquirer*

"SPARKY WHO" SHOWED THEM

Twice named the National League Manager of the Year, Sparky Anderson is the Reds' all-time winningest skipper in the club's history— 863 wins. Nicknamed "Captain Hook" for his quick removal of starting pitchers, Anderson made winning a habit during his tenure in Cincinnati, winning five division titles, four pennants, and two World Series. Fired by the Reds in November 1978, he also won a World Series as the Detroit Tigers' manager in 1984 and was inducted into the Baseball Hall of Fame in 2000. Jim Schottelkotte authored the following article on Anderson for The Cincinnati Enquirer *in 1976.*

One can still remember the cynicism and the doubts that day in October 1969, when George Lee "Sparky" Anderson was introduced as the new manager of the Cincinnati Reds.

"Sparky who?" they laughed. "Can you imagine," said another, "putting this guy in a town that has Bob Cousy and Paul Brown?"

Cousy, one of the great names of basketball, was then trying to rejuvenate the Cincinnati Royals of the National Basketball Association. Brown, who had practically invented modern pro football, was building a new National Football League power with the Cincinnati Bengals.

Sparky Anderson? He was a little-known coach with the San Diego Padres, one of the least regarded teams in baseball; something of a nobody in a short one-year playing career in the major leagues, and with only five years of managing experience in the lower minors. He was replacing Dave Bristol, who had been popular for the most part with the players, and he was taking on a team with its share of big-name stars, few of whom he knew really well and all of whom, presumably, were waiting to be shown.

Sparky Anderson showed them. In a six-year period in which Cousy and the Royals left Cincinnati a failure and in which Brown built skillfully but nevertheless could not win a major championship in football, Sparky Anderson and the Reds won four division titles, three

National League championships, and in 1975 finally grabbed the biggest prize of all, defeating the Boston Red Sox in a tumultuous, dramatic World Series and bringing Cincinnati its first world baseball championship in 35 years.

The statistics are even more impressive. In those six years, Anderson's Reds won 581 games, an average just short of 97 victories a season, and the Reds' winning percentage was .603. Only four other managers in major league history—Frank Chance, Billy Southworth, Al Lopez, and Earl Weaver—did better in their first six seasons.

The beauty of Sparky Anderson is not that record but how unchanged he is from the man who walked into that room at the Netherland Hilton Hotel that day in 1969, wide-eyed, thrilled, and somewhat stunned at his luck in being picked out of nowhere to manage the Reds. From the first, he proved to be a gracious, warm personality, good with the press, good with the fans, and, exactly as Reds' general manager Bob Howsam had predicted, good with the players. His real strength as a manager, say those who observe him, is his sincerity, his honesty, and his ability to communicate with his players.

Says Pete Rose, one of those veterans Sparky had to convince: "I think most of the players would walk through hell in a gasoline suit for him.

"I just think you can talk to him for five minutes and realize he's a sincere guy and down to earth," adds Rose. "He's an honest fellow. He's just a sincere guy."

Rose has played under four managers with the Reds and was invited to make some comparisons.

"Dave [Bristol] was friendly toward the players, too, and, in fairness to Dave, I don't think he's got the players Sparky's got. Dave was a good, hard worker, too. He'd do little things like kicking over food in the clubhouse when he got mad. Sparky wouldn't do things like that. Sparky forgets about it and gets ready for the next game. Sparky is different from Hutch [Fred Hutchinson]. If you got in Hutch's doghouse, he wouldn't say anything. If Sparky gets mad, he'll come and tell you exactly what he thinks you did. If he gets mad, he gets it off his chest and is ready to go.

"He's really involved in the game," adds Rose. "I think he stays ahead of everybody. He's always open for suggestions. The people he's surrounded himself with are another strength. All four of his coaches could be capable managers."

One of those coaches, Alex Grammas, became manager of the Milwaukee Brewers following the 1975 season. Says Grammas:

"I think his big strength is his understanding of people in general and ballplayers in particular and his understanding of the human mind and what makes it tick. That's something you can't reach out and grab. A lot of it has to be in you."

Anderson has always publicly stated managers don't really make that much difference, but Grammas disagrees.

"It's impossible to win without talent," says Grammas. "But if a team is capable of winning 50 games, I think Sparky will win 50. If it's capable of 100, I think he'll win 100."

"He's grown in the job," says Bob Howsam, assessing his manager. "He's as enthusiastic or more so than when I first knew him. He lives and loves baseball, and he's a refreshing type of person in the game because he's so direct in his approach."

Perhaps the reason that Anderson has proved a good manager is that things never came easy for him as a player. It is the fellows who have to dig and scrape out a living as a player who often make the best managers. Bob Howsam agrees.

"I'm firmly convinced of that because I had Ralph Houk for me and Chuck Tanner, Earl Weaver, and Darrell Johnson as well. They were all players who were not outstanding stars. They did it by fighting and clawing their way to the top. They decided in their own minds to learn the game of baseball and qualify themselves to lead."

Certainly that was in Howsam's mind when he settled on George Anderson to lead the Reds. There was another compelling reason why he leaned to Anderson.

"I feel managing in the minors is important. It's not a must but a very important plus. You learn about young players as a whole and you have to do so many more jobs."

What Howsam knew and what the record didn't show was that Anderson had a particular record of success taking young teams, shaping them, and firing them with the will to excel.

"The things that impressed me were his own enthusiasm, his knowledge of the game, and his ability to take a young club and even though it might not be such a good club to begin with because of its youth, in the second half of the season he'd always be up near the top or win with it," recalls Howsam.

And so, October 1969, Sparky Anderson met the press and the doubters. What did the man himself feel?

"I was so naïve and enthusiastic I never looked at what the consequences might be," he says. "I never even thought of what it might be failing. I just thought it was a tremendous opportunity. If I had to start over and knowing what I know now, I'm sure it would be a different feeling. I was just so lucky the way things came off.

"If 1970 [when the Reds won a pennant and got into the World Series against Baltimore] had been 1971 [when the club fell to fourth and won only 79 games], it would have been a nightmare," adds Anderson. "I appreciate that 1970 went so smoothly."

No manager lives without detractors, and those who question Anderson say he simply has more talent than others.

But this is forgetting a masterful job through the years, particularly in 1975, with a pitching staff that has never been completely sound. So often, in fact, did Anderson juggle pitchers in 1975 that he got a new name—Captain Hook.

The name does not appear to bother him because he felt he was consistent with himself and with his players—and he regards that as important.

If he has a strength, he thinks, it is that he always tries to be himself. "I'm kind of a character in that I like to joke with people. I really like people. I don't like to be alone. I think my naturalness with the players has come off. I know they think they can talk with me because I don't make a big to-do about things.

"I don't really have any philosophy. If I have one, I guess it's be yourself. If you're somebody that yells and screams, scream and yell. That's you. Don't try to be something you're not."

There are other things Sparky Anderson believes in that don't get publicity.

"Every homestand, he's always going up to Children's Hospital to see the kids," reveals Rose. "He doesn't do it for publicity.

"He just gives you the impression if you get in trouble at home, he'll help you or listen to you. Most people are afraid to talk to their superiors in that respect."

Roger Kahn, *The New York Times*

ROSE MANAGES HEADFIRST, TOO

In the end, only Pete Rose could stop Pete Rose. Managing the way he played, upon his return to the Queen City in 1984, Rose became the team's player/manager and led the team to four consecutive second-place finishes. Accused of running up enormous gambling debts (and betting on his team) in 1989, the Cincinnati son was eventually banished from the game he loved so much. Roger Kahn profiled the Charlie Hustle style of managing for The New York Times *on May 4, 1987.*

The scene in 1986 was a dark bus splashing through soggy streets in fetid Houston. The Reds had been making a kind of semirun toward the first-place Astros and earlier this day in Cincinnati had thrown their ace, Bill Gullickson, against the Chicago Cubs and a novice pitcher named Greg Maddux.

It looked like a Cincinnati victory until the game began. After three innings, the Cubs were leading by 9–0, baseball's classic forfeit score, and cruised onward, winning, 11–3.

Pete Rose, the manager, took the loss professionally, as is his wont, and on the flight southwest we chatted and played gin rummy. Rose won a few hands, offered his Huck Finn grin, and said, "How come a guy like me, who took five years to get through high school, is beating a guy like you who went to college?" "Never finished." "Deal." A little laughter. But the Reds had dropped a game they expected to win and now they were riding into Houston, home of the Nolan Ryan fastball and the Mike Scott miracle pitch. It would have been better to be entering on a roll.

Suddenly, in the back of the bus, a reserve player began to sing. A few others joined. Rose tapped my knee. "You traveled with Reese and Robinson. Did Reese and Robinson ever sing after they got beat 11–3?" Of course they did not.

"Well, how does this make you feel?" he said.

"Pete, you're the manager. Stand up. Turn on the bus lights. Tell them to shut the hell up."

In the darkness, I could see him shrug. "Wouldn't do any good. Could make it worse. The ballplayers are different these days."

I have been working on a book with Peter Edward Rose since March of 1986, striving not for an "as-I-told-to" cliché, but toward a harmonious blending of our separate voices. Complicated. Enough writer talk. Sometimes I wonder if we are in a collaboration or a marriage, and we each know more about the other than either can ever entirely say.

But I can say that Pete escaped from Montreal, where he was withering, and took over a Cincinnati franchise that had turned so sour there was talk of moving the Reds from the birthplace of professional baseball into that asteroid in New Orleans called the Superdome. Rose pumped blood into the dying beast and brought the Reds home second in each of the last two seasons. (We are here talking about Rose, the manager, but I had better point out that on September 11, 1985, Rose the batsman broke a significant record, set generations earlier by Ty Cobb. The number is 4,192, the most hits made by any major leaguer since the dawn of Cooperstown.) At this writing Rose's Reds have gotten off to a spanking start and, as much as one can handicap such things, seem strong contenders to win the National League West. Rose, whose team makes its first visit to New York to play the Mets tomorrow night, never managed an inning in the minor leagues and says that across most of that magnificent major league playing career he was so concentrated on the business at hand—playing ball—that he thought little about actually becoming a manager himself. "'Cept, of course, I played like a manager."

"Such as."

"Like I always kept my head in the game. Not just my body but my head. My dad, Harry Edward Rose, taught me that. Like I followed the pitching rotation of every other club so I knew who I was gonna hit against 10 days ahead. Like I know you don't make the first out or the last out at third. Like I know how the game's supposed to be played. Like I know a manager who got so sore when his team got beat that he kicked over a couple tables and spilled all the players' food onto the clubhouse floor. I don't think that's particularly smart, because win or lose, your players got to eat."

He plays down his knowledge of the game, sometimes saying: "It's not that complicated. See the ball; hit the ball." But last year, after a game against the Giants, some profundity broke through.

Barry Larkin led off the first inning for the Reds with a squibbing spinner off the end of his bat. Joel Youngblood, at first, played the ball badly and Larkin was credited with a single. Buddy Bell lifted a mighty pop fly, which Youngblood lost in the lights. Another pseudosingle.

Larkin then sprang into a fake steal of third, not the greatest of plays with nobody out. But the fake was so remarkable that Bell, following the lead runner as one should, ran halfway to second base. Larkin returned and there stood Bell, a smart ballplayer, trapped between bases, until Bob Brenly, the Giants' catcher, ran out from his position and tagged him.

"I guess," I said later, "there was nothing Bell could have done but dig a hole in the ground."

"Nothing?" Pete said in mild surprise. "You saw what Youngblood did on the first two plays. I woulda run back to first just to make Joel handle the ball again."

Rose is not much for meetings. He tells his players that he demands only two things: give 100 percent and be on time. But, playing or not, he sets an example with his extraordinary work ethic. He picks up baseballs in the batting cage, something I never saw Stengel or Durocher do. He delegates authority to his coaches, knowing, to be sure, that if the coach can't handle the authority, the coach will be gone. Rose knows who he is, and recognizes that some of the younger players stand in his awe. So he gives them advice most gently. He told a rookie coming up for his first at-bat, "I got something for you, if you want it."

"Yeah," the kid said. "I want it."

"This pitcher's a little wild. Give him a chance to get into a hole." (The end of the story is that the rookie was so nervous that he swung at the first pitch, out of the strike zone, and popped up. Rose took it well, reasoning that the youngster had every right to be nervous.) Can he rip? Last season one of the Reds' outfielders arrived at Riverfront Stadium so dazed that he was unable to put on his uniform. Rose has a little pregame trick. He tramps from his green cement-block office toward the players' lounge, ostensibly to fetch a diet soda. (He drinks no alcohol.) While wandering, he picks up just about everything occurring in the clubhouse.

He noticed the player, approached and sniffed, and, as he says, "no Jack Daniel's." Coming to an unpleasant conclusion, he put an arm around him and guided him into the trainer's room, from which the press is barred. "I'm not exactly in favor of cocaine," Rose said, "but look, I was trying to protect the guy, and anyway, how can you be absolutely sure?"

The next day at Riverfront, the player walked into Rose's office and said, "Sorry, Skipper, I was sick."

Rose's response was hardly printable. He recognizes, as every manager should, that possible cocaine use has become as basic to baseball as the glove, and deals with that rotten reality as best he can.

During the season, Buddy Bell, a poised and charming veteran, would feel even more pain than he did when he found himself at sea between first and second. His year-old daughter Traci underwent open-heart surgery, a procedure that lasted five hours. Rose said:

"Buddy, forget the pennant race. I'm here to worry about that. Go look after your daughter and don't come back till you feel like it."

Bell said: "Then he kinda touched my forearm. Maybe Tommy Lasorda would have hugged me but to tell the truth I didn't feel like being hugged. The touch on the arm, that was just right, and the little girl came through it fine."

Rose deals with each of his players individually. Youngsters like Kurt Stillwell say such things as, "I can't believe I'm actually playing for that man." The fine old hand, Dave Parker, and the manager tease each other, but with affection. Of that sensitive and gifted outfielder, Eric Davis, who doesn't like to be pushed, Rose said: "He can be as good as he wants and make as much money as he wants. It's up to him." Finally, in this year when baseball is being kinder to the memory of Jackie Robinson than the establishment was to the man alive, it seems appropriate to point out that Peter Edward Rose despises racial prejudice. The direct quote is: "There's so much hate in the world as it is; how can you be so stupid as to hate someone because of the color of his skin."

It takes time to know Rose, time to differentiate such things as his grammar, which sometimes slips, from his intelligence, which is as quick as the bat in Pete's playing days of youth and sinew. It takes time to feel the compassion beneath that tough exterior, time, in short, to separate the person from the persona.

When we were getting to know each other he developed a small joke. After a game had gone particularly well and we were alone, Rose would say, "John McGraw?" Not wanting to spoil a national treasure, I'd say, "Not quite." We liked the byplay and kept it going for months.

But seriously, Pete Rose, the Cincinnati kid, as John McGraw? Absurd. And he was not going to break Ty Cobb's record either.

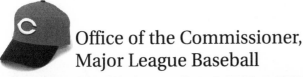

Office of the Commissioner,
Major League Baseball

BARTLETT GIAMATTI STATEMENT ON BANNING PETE ROSE

It wasn't supposed to end, not like this. Pete Rose was banned from baseball for alleged gambling—his managerial career and all other ties to organized baseball were abruptly severed. Baseball Commissioner Bart Giamatti ended the months-long saga with the following statement to the baseball world on August 24, 1989.

The banishment for life of Pete Rose from baseball is the sad end of a sorry episode. One of the game's greatest players has engaged in a variety of acts which have stained the game, and he must now live with the consequences of those acts. By choosing not to come to a hearing before me, and by choosing not to proffer any testimony or evidence contrary to the evidence and information contained in the report of the Special Counsel to the Commissioner, Mr. Rose has accepted baseball's ultimate sanction, lifetime ineligibility.

This sorry episode began last February when baseball received firm allegations that Mr. Rose bet on baseball games and on the Reds' games. Such grave charges could not and must never be ignored. Accordingly, I engaged and Mr. Ueberroth appointed John Dowd as Special Counsel to investigate these and any other allegations that might arise and to pursue the truth wherever it took him. I believed then and believe now that such a process, whereby an experienced professional inquires on behalf of the Commissioner as the Commissioner's agent, is fair and appropriate. To pretend that serious charges of any kind can be responsibly examined by a Commissioner alone fails to recognize the necessity to bring professionalism and fairness to any examination and the complexity a private entity encounters when, without judicial or legal powers, it pursues allegations in the complex, real world.

Baseball had never before undertaken such a process because there had not been such grave allegations since the time of Landis. If one is

141

responsible for protecting the integrity of the game of baseball—that is, the game's authenticity, honesty, and coherence—then the process one uses to protect the integrity of baseball must itself embody that integrity. I sought by means of a Special Counsel of proven professionalism and integrity, who was obliged to keep the subject of the investigation and his representatives informed about key information, to create a mechanism whereby the integrity we sought to protect was itself never violated. Similarly, in writing to Mr. Rose on May 11, I designed, as is my responsibility, a set of procedures for a hearing that would have afforded him every opportunity to present statements or testimony of witnesses or any other evidence he saw fit to answer the information and evidence presented in the Report of the Special Counsel and its accompanying materials.

That Mr. Rose and his counsel chose to pursue a course in the courts rather than appear at hearings scheduled for May 25 and then June 26, and then chose to come forward with a stated desire to settle this matter is now well known to all. My purpose in recounting the process and the procedures animating that process is to make two points that the American public deserves to know:

First, that the integrity of the game cannot be defended except by a process that itself embodies integrity and fairness;

Second, should any other occasion arise where charges are made or acts are said to be committed that are contrary to the interests of the game or that undermine the integrity of baseball, I fully intend to use such a process and procedure to get to the truth and, if need be, to root out offending behavior. I intend to use, in short, every lawful and ethical means to defend and protect the game.

I say this so that there may be no doubt about where I stand or why I stand there. I believe baseball is a beautiful and exciting game, loved by millions—I among them—and I believe baseball is an important, enduring American institution. It must assert and aspire to the highest principles—of integrity, of professionalism of performance, of fair play within it's rules. It will come as no surprise that like any institution composed of human beings, this institution will not always fulfill its highest aspirations. I know of no earthly institution that does. But this one, because it is so much a part of our history as a people and because it has such a purchase on our national soul, has an obligation to the people for whom it is played—to its fans and well-wishers—to strive for excellence in all things and to promote the highest ideals.

I will be told that I am an idealist. I hope so. I will continue to locate ideals I hold for myself and for my country in the national game as well as in other of our national institutions. And while there will be debate and dissent about this or that or another occurrence on or off the field, and while the game's nobler parts will always be enmeshed in the human frailties of those who, whatever their role, have stewardship of this game, let there be no doubt or dissent about our goals for baseball or our dedication to it. Nor about our vigilance and vigor—and patience—in protecting the game from blemish or strain or disgrace.

The matter of Mr. Rose is now closed. It will be debated and discussed. Let no one think that it did not hurt baseball. That hurt will pass, however, as the great glory of the game asserts itself and a resilient institution goes forward. Let it also be clear that no individual is superior to the game.

Fred Mitchell, *Chicago Tribune*

REDS FIND THAT PINIELLA'S WAY WORKS

In 1990, he actually ran onto the field, yanked second base out of the ground, and flung it into the outfield to make a point with an umpire. It didn't matter. Almost everything Lou Piniella did that year worked as he led his Reds on a season-long stint in first place, the first-ever NL team to lead wire-to-wire. The subsequent sweep of the Athletics in the World Series gave Piniella his only world title as a manager. Fred Mitchell authored this profile of the Reds' skipper for the Chicago Tribune *on June 24, 1990.*

The main passage leading into Riverfront Stadium is still Pete Rose Way, the street named after Cincinnati's once-favorite son who was banned from baseball last year.

Longtime residents of this conservative city nestled along the Ohio River were reluctant to castigate Rose, even as the overwhelming evidence poured in that he had broken the national pastime's most sacred commandment: Thou shall not bet on baseball.

But the 1990 Reds have discovered another route to Riverfront Stadium. Instead of Pete Rose Way, these Reds are following Lou Piniella's way and leading the National League West by several car lengths.

"I'm always saying, 'Maybe God sent me Lou.' Then I remember, 'No, George [Steinbrenner] sent me Lou,'" said Reds owner Marge Schott, who gave Piniella a three-year, $1.5 million contract. "So far, I believe in Lou and we have had a good time. Lou told me George used to call him [in the dugout] on the phone all the time. I told Lou not to worry. I will never call him."

Piniella spent the previous 16 seasons with the New York Yankees as a player, coach, manager, general manager, and broadcaster, managing the Yankees in 1986, '87, and part of '88 before Steinbrenner fired him. Piniella must feel as if he has ascended to managerial heaven now that he has escaped Steinbrenner's meddlesome ways.

"In New York, I had a good relationship with George. I respect the guy and I like him. But he's very impatient," said Piniella, choosing his words carefully.

Under Piniella, the Yankees won 90 games in 1986 and 89 in 1987, but they finished second and fourth, respectively, in the competitive American League East.

"Over there, we had good ballclubs when I managed them," he said. "We were short in one very big area, and that was the pitching department. Especially in the summer when the weather got hot and we had an older staff. When they ran out of gas, the club sputtered.

"George either blamed it on the pitching coach or the manager or somebody else. It is much easier to change one person than to change the whole makeup of the ballclub. Here, I was brought in to do a job and the lady [Schott] said that she would not interfere at all. She was going to let me get it done. I am in charge of the personnel here on the field, and I have a very large amount of input on trades.

"It has been very satisfying. I have had no interference at all. If there are problems around here, they are problems that are internal and I can deal with them. They are not external, like they were in New York, where I was caught in the middle as a manager. I've got no complaints here. It has been fun."

Schott's reputation as a sometimes-obtrusive owner did not dissuade Piniella from taking the Reds' job. (She once reportedly thwarted a proposed trade of a popular Reds player because of his community service work in the Cincinnati area.) After all, Steinbrenner's employment of 17 different managers in the last 14 years is the epitome of interference.

"That's the difference between a grand old man of baseball and a woman in baseball," said Schott with a laugh. "I believe in Lou, and he has shown that he can get the job done. We are playing like a team now with enthusiasm. I think that is something I have always believed in. If something serious were to come up, or something I don't like, I let Lou know."

And what does Schott consider serious?

"Being a woman, I am more interested in the example [players and managers] set for children. I think that is terribly important. I have little children who come down to me [in her box seat behind the Reds dugout] who look like they are about three or four years old and they know Chris Sabo and they know Eric Davis. What means the most to me is that our team shows class to the youth, and that is what I would get on Lou's butt about.

"Last time, it was about his language. I got some letters, and I sent him a copy of the letter. It is important because he has to set an example for his players, too."

Considering Rose's seemingly undying legacy in Cincinnati, it might be difficult for this city to embrace Piniella, even if he leads the Reds to the NL pennant.

"They should embrace this team. I couldn't care less if they embrace me or not," said Piniella. "I came in here to get a job done. I am doing that job to the best of my ability. The players are the ones who get the job done on the field. They deserve the credit. I'm here just to direct things and provide some leadership. I am not concerned at all about how they react to me. As long as I get the job done, I will know it."

Reds players were constantly distracted last season because of the investigation of Rose.

"I don't really know what transpired here last year," said Piniella. "I was broadcasting for the Yankees. I told the [Reds] players in spring training that last year was last year and this year is this year. We have a good ballclub, and let's go out and play good baseball. Let's make the other team beat us and not beat ourselves. I know the Reds had injuries last year, too, and that hurt their efforts."

Schott acknowledges the deleterious effect the Rose investigation had on her team.

"It was a very tough thing after we had the Pete and Marge Show for so many years. It was a very difficult situation," said Schott, who was also born in Cincinnati.

"Pete and I were probably the only owner and manager born in the same town. Pete was a hometown hero, and that is why I think this has been so helpful to have Lou come in and win. That should help people put some of these things behind them, because there is no doubt that Pete was the hometown hero.

"People have already said, 'Gosh, Lou is doing a good job.' We picked the right guy, and it wasn't so much a matter of picking because I don't know that many people in baseball. But it is important for the city to see how another man can come in and get the job done."

Reds hitting coach Tony Perez was a friend and former longtime teammate of Rose.

"Last year, in the first two months of the year we were in first place," said Perez. "It looked like the [Rose investigation] didn't bother us, but after that the injuries hit us and everything went downhill. But this year, Lou is keeping everybody together. He runs the show and he is doing a great job."

Through winning, Piniella has also enlisted the support of his players.

"He is a very intense manager," said Sabo. "He wants to win very badly, and it carries over on the bench. He is in every pitch and every game. He is real fun to play for because the guy wants to win big-time.

"It is a lot different this year, of course, because we don't have all the investigation going on with Pete. When you win, everything is great. And when you lose, everything is bad. That's the way sports is. Now that we are winning, everybody likes each other. When you go on a losing streak, everybody wants to hang you. It is something you have to accept, I guess."

Outfielder Billy Hatcher is performing splendidly in the Reds' positive atmosphere.

"I wasn't here last year, but this year it seems like Lou has this team focused," said Hatcher, who was traded from Houston to Pittsburgh to Cincinnati during the off-season.

"Guys are concentrating on baseball, and they are not letting any other activities get in the way of doing their jobs. We are having a lot of fun. We ran into a rough trip on the West Coast where San Francisco beat us three games and then Houston beat us three. But the team kept playing hard. This team just keeps coming back.

"Lou lets me play and steal bases. He tells me to just get on base and not worry about driving in runs. Whatever I drive in is a plus."

Despite their auspicious start, the Reds are keeping the San Francisco Giants and San Diego Padres focused in their rearview mirror.

"We've got good talent here, and we have done some things to improve the ballclub," said Piniella. "Offensively, we have good team speed. We've got some good contact hitting, and we utilize our speed a lot. It is more of a finesse-type offense. It is not a slug-it-out type, although our power is starting to increase.

"We have dependable starting pitching. Jack Armstrong and Tom Browning have both been solid. We have a darn good bullpen, especially with the closers. I'm not surprised that we are in first place. I was somewhat surprised by our 33–12 [record] before we encountered a few problems. We are not a .750 ballclub. I don't think any ballclub is, really."

The Crosley Field scoreboard shows a particularly lopsided score during a Reds game in 1949. The stadium was the team's home for 58 years.

Section IV
THE BALLPARKS

John Erardi, *The Cincinnati Enquirer*

PALACE OF THE FANS

Built on the exact spot of the fire-ravaged League Park, the Palace of the Fans was named as such because it resembled a palace—22 hand-carved Corinthian columns with elaborate detail adorned the top of the grandstand. The strange name for the park never caught on and Reds' fans continued to call the stadium League Park. Opened in 1902, the Palace was home to the Reds until 1911. John Erardi profiled the park for The Cincinnati Enquirer *in its April 1, 1996, edition.*

In three or four years, Cincinnati should have a new ballpark, built for the fans. Ninety-four years ago this month, such a ballpark was unveiled at Findlay and Western avenues in the West End.

It was called the Palace of the Fans at League Park.

Today, we take you back to that Opening Day—Thursday, April 17, 1902—when Cincinnati celebrated the opening of the grandest ball-park ever built.

From his vantage point in right field, young Sam Crawford had a clear view of the word *Cincinnati* chiseled into the frieze atop the Reds' new grandstand called the Palace of the Fans.

Even on this cloudy day, the grandstand shone a milky white against the rich green grass of the infield. The bright red hats and dresses of the women seated in the "fashion boxes"—and the American flags flapping in the breeze—made the grandstand look like a big white deck of peppermint candy.

There were 19 fashion boxes—nine on either side of home plate, and one directly behind it—that ringed the front of the grandstand like opera boxes. In the fashion box directly behind home plate, club owner John Brush, 57, and Indianapolis clothing store owner, turned to an official of the Chicago club.

"What pity it is that all those old stars deserted the National League and killed all the interest in the game!" said Brush.

He was being sarcastic.

Nothing could kill the interest in Opening Day in Cincinnati.

The boxes—and every seat in the ballpark—were filled.

It was 65 degrees, cloudy, with a slight wind out of the northeast. The Ohio Valley was well into spring at 3:00 this afternoon, Thursday, April 17, 1902.

Many fans stood in fair territory along the outfield wall. Total attendance was 10,000, a big turnout. Only 4,800 had turned out for Opening Day the previous year.

The big draw was "The Palace of the Fans."

It was just the second major league grandstand built of concrete and iron. Twenty-two square Corinthian columns, with elaborate detailing at the top, supported the roof.

The seeds for this magnificent structure were planted in Brush's head in 1893, when he attended the World's Fair in Chicago, which reintroduced classical architecture to America. He felt the Beaux Arts style of architecture, a combination of Roman and Greek, would make a wonderful grandstand.

When the old grandstand burned to the ground in 1900, Brush proceeded to build a suitable monument.

Brush hired the Cincinnati architectural firm of Hake & Hake. He wanted to attract the well-heeled burghers as well as the rowdies. In 1901, construction began. On this day, Opening Day 1902, Brush sat in the middle of it.

The temporary covered grandstand in the right-field corner, and the covered pavilion adjacent to the main stands along the right-field line, remained from old League Park. These added another 3,000 seats. Another 4,000 could be accommodated in standing-room-only fashion inside the outfield wall.

Rooters' Row was the section under the fashion boxes, behind home plate. It was on the same level as the field, separated only by a three-foot wooden wall and four feet of chicken wire rising above it. Rooters' Row was for the fans who liked to whoop it up.

It looked like the "Carnivora" building at the Cincinnati Zoo. At the zoo, at least somebody hosed down the inhabitants. Here, the predators went unchecked. Beers were 12 for a dollar. Cigar smoke was thick. Coins and bills changed hands rapidly. Whiskey? You could get it, but only in the bar area outside Rooters' Row, underneath the stands. Big glass containers of hard-boiled eggs and pickles sat atop the bar.

Cold beer, lemonade, "to cool the inner man," candy, and pretzels were hawked by vendors walking through the stands. At the refreshment area, clerks sold ham sandwiches and fat links of German sausages.

The new scorecard was a keeper. A photo of the Palace of the Fans adorned the frontispiece. But some fans looked quizzically at the Reds lineup: Harry Black—who hadn't played in a single exhibition game— was listed as the left fielder.

Among the patrons in Rooters' Row this day was 22-year-old Miller Huggins, a graduate of Walnut Hills High School, who played second base for a local amateur team, St. Paul's.

"*Wahoo Sam!*"

Fans throughout the ballpark—in Rooters' Row, in the fashion boxes, in the seats and benches behind the fashion boxes, in the bleachers in right field—yelled Crawford's nickname as he came to bat in the bottom half of the first inning.

Yahoo for Wahoo

It was the Reds' 19th season at Findlay and Western.

In 1884, the club had turned an abandoned brickyard into a serviceable ballyard. Until 1893, the diamond remained tucked into the corner of Findlay and Western avenues, which put the sun in the hitters' eyes, which was not a good thing. By the time Crawford arrived in September 1899, the diamond had been relocated. The sun was now in the right fielder's eyes—Crawford's eyes—but he could live with that. It was his bat that got him to the big leagues at age 19.

Crawford batted fourth. He had led the league in home runs in 1901 with 16 and hit an equal number of triples while scoring 91 runs and batting in 104. This was his third Opening Day in Cincinnati.

He had come a long way from his boyhood days in Wahoo, Nebraska. He and his friends had fashioned their own baseballs. They'd gather loose string and yarn and "get hold of a little rubber ball for the center." Then they'd get their mothers to sew a cover on the ball.

In 1898, when Crawford turned 18, he and a dozen ballplaying buddies made a trip in a lumber wagon drawn by two horses. One of the boys had talked his father into letting them borrow it. They went from town to town, taking on all comers. Every little town had its own team and its own diamond. In the wagon, one of the boys had a cornet. When the wagon arrived in town, he'd whip out the horn and sound off.

"People would all come out to see what was going on, and we'd announce that we were the Wahoo team and we were ready for a ballgame," said Crawford. "We didn't have any uniforms or anything, just baseball shoes maybe."

The boys from Wahoo were on the road about three weeks.

"Lived on bread and beefsteak the whole time," said Crawford. "We'd take up a collection at the games—pass the hat, you know—and that paid our expenses. Or some of them, anyway. One of the boys was a cook, but all he could cook was round steak. We'd get 12 pounds for a dollar and have a feast.

"We'd drive along the country roads, and if we came to a stream, we'd go swimming; if we came to an apple orchard, we'd fill up on apples. We'd sleep anywhere. Sometimes in a tent, lots of time, out on the ground, out in the open. If we were near a fairgrounds, we'd slip in there. If we were near a barn, well…"

After Wahoo's team beat the team in West Point, Nebraska, Crawford got a call from a manager there. He said they'd pay him, or at least get him a job. Crawford jumped at the chance, and when a team-mate got Sam an opportunity to play for Chatham in the Canadian League in 1899 for $65 a month, Sam jumped again.

That season ended in July, and Crawford was sold to Grand Rapids in the Western League, then to Cincinnati in September.

"So there I was, in 1898 touring Nebraska with the Wahoo team in a wagon, and in 1899 playing in the big leagues with the Cincinnati Reds," marveled Wahoo Sam.

He made $150 a month.

The Reds center fielder was Dummy Hoy, 39, a fleet-footed won-derful-fielding deaf mute, who was in his 13th big-league season.

Hoy had been the Reds center fielder from 1894 to 1897, then rejoined the Reds for this season. Hoy, a wee fellow at 5'5" and 165 pounds, could still giddyap on the basepaths—even though he was only a month short of his 40th birthday. He'd stolen 27 bases in 1901 for the Chicago White Sox, giving him 586 stolen bases.

And he was still a great center fielder.

Crawford had learned Hoy's ways in the exhibition games.

If a batted ball came into an overlapping area in right-center field—where the planks in the fence were painted with the words *Moerlein*, as in *Moerlein Beer, Absolutely Pure*—Crawford would listen up. Hoy couldn't hear, so there was no sense calling for the ball. Hoy couldn't talk, but he could make "kind of a throaty noise, kind of a little squawk."

"When a fly ball came out and I heard this little noise, I knew he was going to take it," said Crawford. "We never had any trouble about who was going to take the ball."

At third base was 24-year-old Harry Steinfeldt, already in his fifth season with Cincinnati. He had made a living performing with Al Field's Minstrels before he entered baseball. The Reds' best pitcher—Noodles Hahn, who won 22 games in 1901 and led the league in innings (375) and complete games (41)—was on the bench. He was not ready to be Opening Day starter.

Brush with Greatness

As owner Brush sat watching his boys play Chicago, he checked the scoreboard for the New York Giants game. He hoped to own the Giants some day; his daughter, Eleanor, wanted to be in the theater, and there was no better place for that than New York.

He liked Cincinnati—well, not enough to live here, no—but he felt a kinship with the fans.

He loved Opening Day. It was a marketer's dream.

And Brush was a marketer.

League Park was well-served by streetcars. Train tracks bordered the western edge of the park. Brush still remembered Opening Day in 1893. About 50 men and boys were sitting atop freight cars enjoying their free view of the game when a locomotive backed up and hooked up to the cars. Away went the train up the Mill Creek—fans and all—as Brush and the paying spectators inside the park chortled.

In 1894, Brush erected a new wood and iron grandstand and moved the diamond to the southwest corner of the grassy expanse—the same place where it was located when the Palace of the Fans opened.

Although the fence along Findlay Avenue was 12 feet high, people would occasionally try to scale it. On Opening Day 1894, a well-dressed man tried, but an usher pushed him back over to the street. The man's fall was broken when he landed on the back of a policeman.

Such shenanigans always escalated on Opening Day, when fans filled streetcars to overflowing and joined in impromptu parades from downtown to the ballpark. Opening Day 1895 was marred by the death of a streetcar rider who hung from the side of an overcrowded car, brushed against a fence, and tumbled under the wheels.

Brush wasn't blamed for that, though the press was not thrilled with him for being an absentee landlord—even though he attended a lot of games.

His players respected him, even if they didn't love him.

Mixing Business with Pleasure

Like all the baseball club owners, Brush was a penny-pincher when it came to player salaries.

On the road, most owners quartered their players in cheap hotels and made them travel by day coach for trips under 300 miles. Brush tried to make sure his players traveled in style—in Pullman cars, at first-class hotels—but conditions could still be tough.

"We had sleeper trains in 1899 and 1900," said Crawford, "but the sleepers had gaslights in them, not electric lights. They used to go around and light them up at night.... The hotels weren't the best in the world, and the trains had coal-burning engines. So, you'd wake up in the morning covered with cinders. They had fine little screens on the train windows, but the cinders would still come through."

Brush did what he could.

He believed in attracting a mix of people to the ballpark, making sure there was something for everyone. He was a family man, and a man of the people.

He criticized other owners for tending "to keep baseball in the saloon class."

The emphasis at the Palace of the Fans was not on the players—who had to sit on benches on the field, instead of in dugouts. The visitors had to dress at their hotel before the game. There was no locker room for them. They came to the ballpark on trolley cars or horse-drawn wagons.

Brush enjoyed baseball...and making money. Orphaned at four, he grew up in Clintonville in northern New York. He and his brother, George, slept in their grandparents' unheated barn because there wasn't room in the house.

Brush worked on the family farm until he was 12, became a clerk in a country store in Clintonville, then worked in a clothing store in Utica (where he became a fan of the Troy Haymakers baseball team, an archrival of the Cincinnati Red Stockings of 1869). Backed by this Utica clothing firm, he moved to Indianapolis to open a store in 1875 at age 30.

In Indy, he built a diamond and organized a semipro club, then attracted an American Association team in 1884 (the AA was a major league). Brush saw baseball as a way to sell "ready-made" suits for boys and men at his department store. Once each home series, he hired a band to give a concert, leather cushions were provided for the ladies, and thousands of cardboard fans bearing an ad for his department store were passed out to the crowd.

Indy was dropped from the league in 1886. When the St. Louis National League club went to auction in August 1886, Brush bought it and moved it to Indy. Brush dug up his old diamond, installed drainage pipes and 18 inches of top soil, and created a stadium that was the envy of the league.

He drove his horse and carriage out near the left-field foul line and gave some youngster free admission to the game if the lad would watch the boss's rig.

"Let her range along here, but don't let her get in the fielder's way," said Brush.

To spur public interest in baseball in Indy, Brush had built a special box for celebrity guests—such as James Whitcomb Riley, Benjamin Harrison, authors Booth Tarkington and Meredith Nicholson, and actors Nat Goodwin and Henry Dixie.

Brush tried to introduce the first black man to major league baseball: J.W. "Bud" Fowler, a sure-fielding second baseman from a nearby minor league. But there was resistance from the league and Fowler was never signed.

In 1890, the league dropped Indianapolis. Brush sold some of his players to the New York Giants for $60,000 ($20,000 in cash, the rest in stock), then bought the Reds in the spring of 1891...and held on to his Giants stock.

Trolley-Car Parade

Crawford settled in at home plate.

A few hours earlier, he and his teammates had gathered at the ball-park, changed into their new white and red uniforms, and boarded the trolley at half past 12 and headed for Fountain Square to meet the Chicago team.

The Chicagos were staying at the Burnet House downtown. Manager Frank Selee and his players had arrived by train in the morning from Champaign, Illinois, where they were training with the University of Illinois team.

Separate trolley cars paraded the Reds and Cubs through town, past Straus' store at 415 Vine Street, where tickets were on sale for 50 and 65 cents.

The two teams were accompanied by Weber's Military Band, belting out march tunes as bystanders shouted to the players, "Bring home a winner, boys!"

Electric trolleys were the way most people got to the ballpark. There were 210 miles of street railway service in Cincinnati, logging 53,000 miles a day; 430 cars passed Fountain Square every hour.

A few people came to the ballpark in carriages pulled by horses. Fewer still rode in the new horseless carriages. Some people walked. Any groups who wanted to parade on the field and honk horns before the game could do so. Plenty did. Two hours before the game, the out-field resembled a street carnival.

The trolley-car parade of ballplayers and the band reached the Palace of the Fans at 2:00 P.M., an hour before game time. The fans all rose in cheer when both teams entered.

On the field in foul territory outside first base, the band sat and played an hour-long concert while the players warmed up.

A *Cincinnati Enquirer* reporter, after circulating through the fans, typed these words for the next day's newspaper: "The office boy rubbed elbows with the millionaire banker.... The crowd was a living demonstration of what a ball team is worth to a city, for in it were people from no less than 50 of Cincinnati's sister cities and villages in the three states, and even as far away as West Virginia—three rooters from Charleston, who didn't want their names mentioned, had reserved seats in the grandstand."

Curtain Goes Up

Wahoo Sam went 0-for-3.

The Reds lost, 6–1.

But before he left for Indianapolis that night, Brush said he was thrilled by the Opening Day crowd at the new Palace.

"The proof of popular interest in the game—and the team—was certainly offered in today's grand outpouring," said Brush.

That night at the Burnet House, Cubs manager Selee was in a cheerful mood, taunting Reds manager Bid McPhee's choice of Len Swormstedt as his starting pitcher. Swormstedt, 22, was a Cincinnati native.

"I've got a squad of bad-winged youngsters," he said. "But if Len Swormstedt is the best McPhee has on tap, I guess Cincinnati has some pitchers in just as bad a shape as I do. Swormstedt didn't show us anything this afternoon."

Lost in Time

In August 1902—only four months after the Palace of the Fans had opened—Brush sold the Reds and the ballpark to the Cincinnati gin and yeast kingpins, Julius and Max Fleischmann, and political bosses George Cox and August "Garry" Herrmann for $150,000. The New York Giants were for sale, and Brush's daughter was anxious to get to Broadway. Brush bought the Giants for $100,000. He and manager John McGraw combined to bring New York four pennants and a world championship in 1905.

Charles Comiskey in Chicago and Philip Shibe in Philadelphia tried to imitate in their cities Brush's flamboyance with the Palace of the Fans, but neither came close. Under Brush's leadership, the Giants built the Polo Grounds, which was regarded as "the magnificent stadium" at the time of his death in 1912 at age 67.

In 1906, the Reds owners added a wooden upper deck to the top of the Palace. By 1907, the nonconcrete portion of the ballpark—not the Palace of the Fans grandstand—was in need of repair. The grandstand, even with the deck added atop it, could not seat enough people. Baseball attendance around the country was booming—but not in Cincinnati because there weren't enough seats.

After the 1911 season, wrecking crews tore down the Palace—it was only 10 years old—and the rest of League Park. Quickly in the off-season the Reds built a bigger park—Redland Field, which later became known as Crosley Field.

On Opening Day 1912, fans set a Cincinnati attendance record of 26, 336. Every seat was filled; the entire perimeter of the field, in fair and foul territory, was four to six fans deep, sitting and standing.

Crawford led the league in triples (23) in 1902, when the Reds finished in fourth place, 70–70. He jumped to Detroit of the American League for the 1903 season, where Ty Cobb later joined him in the Tigers outfield. Crawford played 15 seasons in Detroit. He still holds the major league record for career triples (312). He was elected to the Hall of Fame in 1957, and died in 1968 at age 88.

His Reds' outfield mate, Hoy, played his final big-league season in 1902. He died in Cincinnati in December 1961, at age 99.

Swormstedt, the Opening Day pitcher in 1902, went 0–2 that season. He jumped to Boston in the AL in 1903, went 1–1, and was done with his big-league career at age 24.

Michael Gershman wrote in his 1993 book, *Diamonds: The Evolution of the Ballpark*, that "Brush clearly created the first major-league ballpark with a distinct architectural style.... He created the first baseball palace."

There has never been a ballpark so magnificent.

"If I could go back in time to visit one old-time ballpark," said Gershman, "the Palace of the Fans would be it."

Sources: *The Cincinnati Enquirer*, April 11–19, 1902; Sam Crawford interview in *The Glory of Their Times*, by Lawrence S. Ritter; *Diamonds: The Evolution of the Ballpark*, by Michael Gershman; *The Cincinnati Game*, by John Baskin and Lonnie Wheeler; *The Sporting News*, *Indianapolis Star*, and *Sporting Life* articles on former Reds owner John Brush, provided by Mr. Grace; *Crosley Field, The Illustrated History of a Classic Ballpark*, by Greg Rhodes and John Erardi; *The Cincinnati Reds*, by Lee Allen; *Souvenir Book of the National Association of Master Bakers Convention, Cincinnati, 1902*; *Book of the Businessman's Club of Cincinnati, 1902*; *Baseball: An Illustrated History*, by Geoffrey C. Ward and Ken Burns; *Cincinnati: The Queen City*, by Daniel Hurley; *Cincinnati: Then and Now*, by Iola Silberstein; *Cincinnati*, WPA Guide; *The Baseball Encyclopedia*, edited by Joseph Reichler.

Souvenir Program

DEDICATION OF THE PALACE OF THE FANS GRANDSTAND

The souvenir program from the Dedication of the Grandstand included statements and sentiments from Cincinnati's newspapers: the Times-Star, *the* Enquirer, *and the* Post.

We are gathered here today to dedicate the most magnificent structure of its kind in the world. This pretty and massive crescent of concrete, iron, and steel will shelter thousands of the great Middle West after many of us have passed away. It will long tower as a fitting monument to the intrepid business acumen of two sportsmen—Mr. John T. Brush and Mr. N. Ashley Lloyd. Viewed from the standpoint of a practical art, it is difficult to imagine anything more beautiful and durable. Would it be too fanciful to compare it with the great architectural structures, which, by their massive strength, have managed to survive the ravages of barbarism and the wrecks of time in the centuries now dead? Bring forth an Egyptian obelisk—with its quaint Oriental Hieroglyphics— and within its falling shadow start the murmuring of a sweet-voiced fountain—and the effort is easy to conjure the pristine conception of the Moorish Courts of the Alhambra. Viewed even as the miniatured sextant, is it not aptly suggestive of the greatest amphitheater the genius of man ever designed and today the King of Ruins—the Colosseum of Rome? True it is the extant ruins of the once majestic and gigantic monument of the ancient Roman arena, where the gladiatorial contests were held, were commonly visited by 87,000 spectators. With due respect for mathematical proportions the kindred association of ideas is nevertheless easily accounted for, and in the camera of the local admirer of the "Palace of the Fans" may be aptly developed a ready vision of the ancient Flavian arena—even though it be diminished to the undersize of a dim perspective.

It would not be surprising if Billy Hoy's first glaring error of the season would be attributed to this composite picture of vision and historical memory. As he relieves his fidgety action of covering the man at the bat with a furtive glance at this luminous grandstand with its mass of swaying fans, or restless quitters—will not the mute's quick activity of thought find facile transition to the scene of the old Roman holiday?

While "Noodles" Hahn, the king of southpaws—past or present— is effectively taking the tantalizing measure of Van Haltern, Doyle, Brodie, or Lauder, and force an act that brought fame and fortune to Gus Hill—club swinging—may not our brilliant and pensive center fielder draw the mental picture of 20 centuries ago as he is absorbed in the study of this great grandstand?

"Rooters' Row" seems to sink below the diamond now trans-formed into the historical arena—and memory traces the dens for the wild beasts (no allusions to rooters)—while the massive columns that here and there obstruct so teasingly the rooters' vision seem to be canopied into corridors through which the lions rushed to the open arena.

Higher up in the grandstand the rows of mighty arches lead to the highest tiers, where thousands of men and women intent upon the combat, are glaring with bated breath at the unequal issue of beast and Christian in the arena below.

Again change the mute's position. See the speechless determina-tion in his wizard face, as he stands at the bat and turns to see Heiney Peitz elevate his right or left hand, signaling that the umpire has called a strike or a ball. And is not the old Colosseum day renewed as in fancy we see the victor pausing before inflicting the fatal below to read the verdict of the populace, while the victim likewise lifts his hand in piteous appeal for life. Alas—the thumbs of the Roman Emperor, of the Roman matrons, of the Roman cowards are turned downward— the gladiator must die, Bob Emslie has just shouted: "Three strikes, you're out!"

To our guests of today—the New York Giants—we bid welcome. We hope you will succeed against all clubs save our own Reds. To Mr. Andrew Freedman and his friends, and to other National League pres-idents, we extend greetings.

Baseball is greater than all outdoor sports combined. It is more widely read and talked about than any other sporting topic. It is little wonder then that Messrs. Brush and Lloyd should spend a fortune in erecting a suitable grandstand in which enthusiasts may comfortably view their favorite game. Time will show the wisdom of their action. Other such structures will be built around the circuit ere long and the score-card vendors will be able to emulate the example of the young Cincinnatian, who exclaimed on Opening Day: "Ain't it a peach!"

The Times Star. **Chase W. Murphy.**

The National Game Immortal

It must be owned that the gentlemen who control the destines of base-ball have acted badly at times—that occasionally a season comes that sees an act or acts committed that are not relished by the patrons of the game. In the National League, within my recollection, there have been the revolt of the players in 1890; the troubles over Harry Stovey and Louis Bierbauer that led to the war between the National League and the old American Association in 1891; the so-called farming evil, "rowdy baseball," as tolerated by the club owners on their individual teams; the differences of opinion among certain magnates, whose names need not be introduced, now that all are up to the ears with each other in the clear, sweet waters of peace; the break between the National and the American Leagues, which was followed by the whole-sale raids on the National League players, who at least were morally bound to the older organization; the split in the National last year, when the contest was between an alleged trust scheme—which was never formally launched—and the placing of the affairs of the league into the hands of Mr. A.G. Spalding, who has since demonstrated that he is an erratic genius, to say the least; and lastly, the troubles of the American League in the courts in suits filed by the National.

These and other occurrences have in their day called forth the wail from the pessimist that "the magnates are killing the game." The idea has been proved most fallacious on many occasions—and never more so than this season, which, so far, has been the most prosperous in years—if not in the history of the game—and this, too, in the face of the fact that the club owners of the National League still were at log-gerheads a month before the season opened, and it was predicted far and wide that by their actions they had killed the game.

Club owners, members of organized baseball associations, may kill themselves baseballically speaking, by acts that are contrary to public opinion and public desire. But the game itself grows stronger each year.

Where one man may lose interest in the game, and remain away from the contests, there are five new and enthusiastic recruits to offset his desertion. One of the earliest toys an American boy receives is a ball of some kind. In time he learns to catch and throw it. As he mingles with boys of his age, even before he goes to school, tossing a ball is one of his chief amusements. His knowledge of handling the ball increases with practice and by watching his elder brothers play. Eventually he is pressed into service in a game that is short a player or two. He becomes more expert, and his love for the game increases with each succeeding summer month. He plays every year, until business pre-vents him indulging in his favorite game. Then he does the next best thing—he goes to games; and if those of the professional players do not suit him, or the management of these teams displeases him, he seeks amateur contests, and derives much satisfaction from them. He seldom or never goes alone, frequently taking with him one of the few who have not had his early training in baseball, these, including the ladies, who are yearly becoming better patrons of the games, and make "fans" of them.

No, the National game cannot be killed. It is immortal. It is the game of the people, the club owners simply acting as the agents of the public in providing the sport. Magnates may come, and magnates may go, but baseball goes on forever.

Sporting Editor, The Times-Star.

From Cradle to Palace

Cincinnati is the birthplace of professional baseball, and the Queen City of the West, which provided the cradle for the National game, has seen the Palace of the Fans rise in all its architectural grandeur—a lasting tribute to the sport that arouses all that is good in loyal, ambitious American hearts. There have been but few breaks in the line of succession since the Cincinnati Red Stockings were organized on July 23, 1866. The Reds of today are the heirs of the sportive spirit then made manifest, and that heritage has grown with the years until now Cincinnati is rated one of the most enthusiastic of Balldom's populous centers.

A.B. Champion was the first president of the Cincinnati Club, with E.E. Townley, treasurer, and John P. Joyce, secretary, and among its sponsors were men who have figured largely in the political and mercantile history of Ohio's chief metropolis. Gen. Andrew Hickenlooper, Leon Van Loo, John R. McLean, Bellamy Storer, John L. Stettinius, A.G. Corre, H.C. Yergason, George B. Ellard, William Worthington, Drausin Wulsin, J.J. McDowell—these are but a few of those on the roster of original stockholders, while A.T. Goshorn, N.L. Anderson, ex-Mayor S.S. Davis, A.D. Bullock, and ex-Congressman Job E. Stevenson, who have scored their last home runs in the game of life, were also numbered with the earliest fathers of the Red Stockings.

When that team took the field nearly 36 years ago, Harry Wright was pitcher, and L.L. Douglass, catcher, and the other members were Charles H. Gould, first base; Asa Brainard. second base; Fred Waterman, third base; J.C. How, shortstop; J.V.B. Hatfield, left field; Rufus King, middle field; and J. William Johnson, right field, with Moses Grant, substitute. In '66 that team played but four games—won two and lost two. In '67 the Reds won 16 games and lost one, and in '68 won 41 and lost six. Then came the never-to-be-equaled record of '69, when the all-conquering tour of the country was made. Harry Wright drew $28.50 a week from the Cincinnati Club, and was the first salaried ballplayer in the world. Modern salary lists, running far into the tens of thousands, are figurative proofs of the game's growth. The Nursery of '66 is only a reminiscence. The Palace of 1902 a magnificent reality.

Baseball Editor, The Cincinnati Enquirer.

The Connecting Link: The Game—the Press—the People

It is a broad statement to make, but nevertheless the truth, the great National game of the United States has the newspapers of the country to thank for its success, totally and entirely. The press took hold of it when it was but a babe in swaddling clothes, tenderly cared for it in its infancy, trained it in its early youth, and now in its majority looks after it with a careful eye, and guides it critically over the stormy road it has to travel.

Will it ever grow old?

Never! It ages, like all things, as time flies, but never grows old. The rejuvenating power of the printing press is behind it and prevents that which characterizes animal life in advancing years. But it would grow old, decrepit, die, and be forgotten in a very short space of time if the newspaper world would deny to it the support now given. It would return to that stage of "infancy" where it was when the press took a hold of it and raised it to its present high pinnacle of success.

The press has made baseball possible. Day after day the recording of contests all over the country goes on. At the outset the space given was meager; but it was a "poor man sport" and the common people were interested. Little by little it grew as the newspapers published accounts of games. Leagues were formed and professional clubs were supported on every side. At home and abroad the work of these traveling bands of players was followed, this made possible by the published telegraphic reports, and now the most important section of the daily newspaper to the hundreds of thousands of "fans" the country o'er is the "Baseball News." Expert views on players and their methods are eagerly read. Every item of information is snapped up with an avidity that is astonishing, and through this worked sentiment the game goes on and on, increasing in popularity as times flies.

Without the support of the press the game could not live. Without the support of the press the people would not want it. Cut out the connecting line and all would be over from a baseball standpoint, and there would be no further user for the Palace of the Fans.

Sporting Editor, The Post.

Lou Smith, *Sport* magazine

CROSLEY FIELD

The Reds' home park for 58 years, Crosley Field was erected at the same location as its predecessor, Palace of the Fans. Originally called Redland Field, the stadium became Crosley Field in 1934 when Powel Crosley purchased both the team and the stadium. The Reds played their final game in Crosley on June 24, 1970. Sport *magazine ran Lou Smith's article on Crosley Field in its March 1953 issue.*

Ten years is a long time to wait! Cincinnati baseball fans waited that long to see a fair ball hit over the fence for a home run at Crosley Field. Cincinnati, of course, is the cradle of professional baseball. Lincoln Park, where the Reds first played, rates that honor. But professional baseball was still in the diaper stage early in the 1880s when the Reds moved to their present location, which was then a brickyard at Western and Findlay avenues, and called Redland Field. The name was changed to Crosley Field when Powel Crosley Jr. took over the ownership of the Cincinnati club in 1934. The park seats 30,101.

The grandstand now used at Crosley Field was first opened to the public in 1912—and it was then that the Cincinnati fans had to wait 10 years to see their first home run hit over the outfield wall. The first fair ball hit over the left-field fence at Crosley field in a championship game was hit by Louis Baird "Pat" Duncan of the Reds, on June 2, 1921, off Marvin Mardo Goodwin of the St. Louis Cardinals. The first fair ball exploded into the right-field bleachers was hit by outfielder Walton E. Cruise of the Boston Braves on June 17, 1922. In 1921, Babe Ruth clouted two home runs at Redland Field, one, a towering shot over the center-field fence, and the other into the bleachers.

In 1938, Warren Giles, then general manager of the Reds, moved home plate up more, cutting 11 feet off the distance to left and right fields and 20 feet off the distance to center field. Before the position of the plate was changed at Crosley Field and the seats near the foul lines eliminated, it was possible to bounce home runs into the left- and right-field pavilions. On September 4, 1927, Lloyd "Little

Poison" Waner of the Pittsburgh Pirates, sliced a low liner over third that hopped crazily into the low seats in left field, just beyond the 250-foot mark. It was scored as a homer. His brother, Paul "Big Poison" Waner, followed with an identical drive over third that went for a second fluke homer. This led to a change in the National League rules, which made any ball that bounced over a barrier a ground-rule double.

Giles, in 1945, hoping to increase home-run production at the park, erected a screen in right field in front of the regular bleacher fence, which shortened the distance to the stands from 366 to 342. This was promptly nicknamed "Giles' Chicken Run," and remained in effect until the 1950 season, when it was returned to its original distance. Last winter it was trimmed to 342 again to "enhance the confidence of our left-handed batters."

The distances to the fences at Crosley Field are now 342 to right field, 328 to left, and 387 to center field.

Crosley Field also has been the scene of many thrilling innovations that have augmented the national pastime. Since the late Franklin Delano Roosevelt threw the switch in the White House that illuminated Crosley Field in 1935 for the first major league night baseball game, baseball under the lights has become a standard big-league feature. The first play-by-play broadcast of a major league game at Crosley Field was made by owner Powel Crosley Jr., who aired the opening game of the 1927 season over station WLW.

A prevailing wind blows in at Crosley Field, which makes it anything but a home-run-hitter's paradise. Hank Sauer, now with the Chicago Cubs, holds the Reds' home-run record for right-handed batters at 35. He hit 22 of these at Crosley Field. Ival Goodman still owns the record for left-handed hitters, walloping 30 in 1938 for the Reds, 15 into the distant right-field bleachers.

Crosley Field has long proven to be a nemesis for Ralph Kiner. The Pirates slugger has hit 294 homers in seven years in the league, but only eight of them have been at Crosley Field.

The heartbreaks and poignant memories wrapped in the shadows of Crosley Field are without number and stretch over a long period of years. The last game pitched by the great Cy Young was at Crosley Field in 1911. The last time that Lou Gehrig donned a Yankees uniform was for the fourth and final game of the 1939 World Series at Crosley Field, although the immortal Iron Man had already retired from the playing field. Johnny Vander Meer pitched the first of his two consecutive no-hitters in 1938 on the Cincinnati mound.

Crosley Field has also produced its share of zany incidents, as it was here in the record flood of 1937 that the irrepressible left-hander, Lee Grissom, rowed a boat over the center-field fence in search of the pitcher's mound covered by 40 feet of muddy Ohio River water. The Redleg park was also the scene of Ernie Lombardi's celebrated "swoon" in the tenth inning of the fourth game of the 1939 World Series against the Yankees—which the Reds lost.

All this has gone toward making Crosley Field one of baseball's most historic stadiums.

John Erardi, *The Cincinnati Enquirer*

COME FULL CIRCLE

The third cookie-cutter stadium to open in the country, Riverfront was the first ball field to be entirely covered with AstroTurf, save the areas around the bases and home plate. Another interesting note on the stadium is that construction on its press area and stadium club were never completed. In 1997, the stadium was renamed Cinergy Field for the Cincinnati-based Cinergy Corporation. John Erardi authored the Riverfront profile "Come Full Circle" for The Cincinnati Enquirer *on June 25, 2002.*

For what Riverfront Stadium was intended to do—stimulate a city, clean up a riverfront, attract a pro football franchise, and keep the Reds in town by giving them a spacious new home with great access and plenty of parking—it worked.

And worked well.

"There was no reason to think it wouldn't serve twice as long as it has (33 seasons)," said former Mayor Gene Ruehlmann, who along with the late Governor Jim Rhodes was in the vanguard of getting the deal done. "It was state-of-the-art. We had carefully looked at other stadiums. But circumstances change."

The change was in the amount of money that could be generated by luxury suites and other features of a new stadium that draw big crowds and more dollars. The result is that circumstances rendered a stadium obsolete before its infrastructure did.

"I wish we could move it to the Dominican instead of having to knock it down," Reds pitcher Jose Rijo said. "That seems like such a waste of a big stadium that still is so useful."

Many Cincinnatians have similar feelings. But with progress, you either keep up with it or you get buried by it. And such was the case when the baseball purists in the mid-1960s were pushing for building a baseball-only facility.

Progress argued against it.

Reds radio broadcaster Waite Hoyt, whose voice and stories were every bit as intimate as the ballpark (Crosley Field) in which he told them, put it this way:

"The moment you enter Riverfront Stadium or Three Rivers Stadium you feel like you're witnessing an exhibition, a spectacle. It's like a giant coliseum. You feel alone."

And Cincinnati wasn't alone in breaking ground for a circular, multipurpose stadium in 1968.

Between the time Dodger Stadium was built in 1962 in Los Angeles and the new Comiskey Park in Chicago in 1991, only one new stadium was built for baseball only: Royals Stadium (1973) in Kansas City.

In a chapter titled "Domes and Concrete Doughnuts" in the bible of ballpark history, *Diamonds,* author Michael Gershman wrote that "safety and security" were the watchwords for these 1970s-era stadiums.

"These parks, built in an age of anxiety, were designed to minimize uncertainties of all kinds—bad hops in the infield, crazy bounces in the outfield," Gershman wrote. "In place of uncertainty, there was 'entertainment'—gigantic scoreboards that featured blowups of players' faces, sing-alongs, and exhortations such as Chaaaarge!!!!!"

Sound familiar?

Anybody who had ever been to Crosley Field, or even a minor league ballpark, knew that while they were watching baseball at Riverfront Stadium, they did not feel like a part of it the way they had in these other cozy settings.

In this sense, Riverfront Stadium didn't work for baseball as well as a baseball-only park would have. But given what he had to work with—and by no means was he complaining—Reds general manager Bob Howsam, his front-office staff, and the Big Red Machine did more than put Cincinnati back on the baseball map.

They made it the capital of Baseball Nation, which Cincinnati hadn't been since founding the pro game in 1869.

And city fathers paved the way without a sales tax.

Riverfront Stadium's $44 million cost was financed through the sale of bonds. The bonds, and the interest on them, were paid off by a 25-cent surcharge on each ticket. Parking revenues and a sizable share of the concessions also went to the city.

"Riverfront Stadium was intended to pay for itself, and it did," Ruehlmann said. "It definitely served its purpose, both from a holistic approach, given its athletic image [the Reds playing in five World Series and winning two of them and the Bengals playing in two Super Bowls] as well as in a cultural and corporate image of a metropolitan area having the things it should [such as a museum, symphony, and zoo]."

With the opening of the stadium as an anchor, development of the central riverfront soon followed: the Coliseum in 1975, Yeatman's Cove and the Serpentine Wall in 1976, Sawyer Point Park in 1978. Residential living returned when One Lytle Place opened in 1980.

Although there was some talk that the stadium would create spinoff development around it, mostly it was intended to clean up the city's front porch, revitalize the city's image, and give some stimulus to downtown. And it did those things, although perhaps not as much as it would have if the expressway between downtown and the stadium wasn't like a moat protecting a castle.

Bob Howsam, son of a Denver beekeeper and honey producer, was not involved in the initial design of Riverfront.

But the Reds' general manager was involved in the evolution of the stadium's baseball features:

He eliminated the order for a Plexiglas screen behind home plate like Crosley Field's. "It blocks out the sound, which is a big part of fan enjoyment," Howsam said.

He brought the bullpens onto the playing field in foul territory. "We made a mistake in putting the bullpens out of sight at Busch Stadium in St. Louis. As soon as the fans see a pitcher warming up, they all become instant managers."

He introduced the first all-AstroTurf infield to the major leagues, leaving dirt only for the batter's box, pitcher's mound, and sliding-pit cutouts around the bases.

"As far as having AstroTurf on the basepaths, I did that because I liked the uniformity of play," Howsam said. "You knew what to expect. You didn't doctor the field. You let your players' abilities [shine]."

National League officials didn't like the idea of a mostly AstroTurf field because it ran contrary to what baseball fields had looked like for as long as anybody could remember.

When the officials came in that first night, "their eyes were glaring," Howsam recalled.

"I liked Warren Giles, but he didn't like the field when he first saw it," Howsam said of the then-NL president. "He told me we had 30 days to see if it worked, and if it didn't, he wanted it out. Well, it worked just fine."

Howsam built a speedy club for the fast AstroTurf, which turned out to be every bit as valuable in attracting fans.

AstroTurf all but guaranteed the show would go on—no matter what the sky looked like when Family of Four stuck its heads out the windows back home in Lexington, Louisville, Indianapolis, Columbus, and Dayton (and even Huntington and Charleston, West Virginia).

The Reds went eight years (August 30, 1978) before they had to issue a rain check.

"It allowed our players to maintain momentum as a team because they knew we were always going to play," Howsam said. "And it allowed fans to make the trip because they knew we were going to play, too."

And how about this stat:

"People talk about what a great year we had in 1976," Howsam said of the 2.63 million in attendance, still the franchise record, "but did you know that if we had a grass field that season, we wouldn't have been able to play at least 22 games, and possibly as many as 29?"

Those games would have been rained out.

Not only did the Reds' 2.63 million lead the majors that year, it was the fourth highest attendance in history. All this from a team in a city that was the second smallest metropolitan market in the majors.

One of Howsam's favorite moments as Reds GM was watching the droves of people teem across the pedestrian walkway and the plaza level toward the stadium with their umbrellas up and open and shielding the rain.

"I wished I'd had somebody take a picture of that," he said.

The U.S. Postal Service won't be issuing any commemorative stamps of the "Great Cereal Bowl Stadiums" of the late 20th century, the way it did in 2001 to honor Crosley Field and eight other ballparks in a series called "Baseball's Legendary Playing Fields."

Crosley Field, Riverfront's predecessor, was one of a handful of ballparks that architects studied before designing Baltimore's gem of a stadium, Camden Yards, which opened in 1992.

But because Riverfront wasn't Crosley is precisely what helped Reds attendance soar in the 1970s. Riverfront had just what the city needed to house the Reds and Bengals: two interstate highways with access ramps, pedestrian walkways from downtown, plenty of safe, well-lit parking escalators, and—for the times—big and clean bathrooms and concession stands.

And it was new, something Crosley Field hadn't been since April 11, 1912, three days before the Titanic sank.

"There's a love affair with a new stadium for three or four years," Howsam said. "We did better than that."

Check out the increase in Reds home attendance from the 1960s, when they were at Crosley Field, to the 1970s, when they were in Riverfront:

1965: 1.05 million
1966: .74 million
1967: .96 million
1968: .73 million
1969: .99 million
1970: 1.80 million (36 games at Crosley Field, 45 at Riverfront)
1971: 1.50 million
1972: 1.61 million
1973: 2.02 million
1974: 2.16 million
1975: 2.32 million
1976: 2.63 million
1977: 2.52 million
1978: 2.53 million
1979: 2.36 million

What Richie Hebner said was true. Inside Riverfront Stadium, you couldn't tell which city you were in.

But Riverfront Stadium did give Cincinnati the "look" it wanted: clean, crisp, and futuristic.

And the lighting was a huge part of it.

It was the stadium's best feature. It still is.

Shortly after Atlanta-based architects George T. Heery and Bill Finch were awarded the contract to codesign Riverfront Stadium, they spoke to the *Enquirer*. Heery said a series of tiered lights would form an unbroken band around the topmost rim that "will, in effect, be a crown of light," a marked improvement over any other stadium, all of whose lighting was "not very attractive."

The most stunning photos taken of the Queen City are at night, featuring the downtown skyline, stadium, and John A. Roebling Suspension Bridge all lit up.

This combination remains a redeeming quality 32 years after the stadium opened. It is Cincinnati.

"Viewed alone, these concrete doughnuts can be numbingly bland...yet in context with the Suspension Bridge...Riverfront seems a natural part of its surroundings," Gershman wrote.

A glimmer of praise.

But for the guy running the show all those years, his review is as bright as a sparkling gem.

"I loved it," Howsam said. "It meant a lot to the fans and to the city. It was just what we needed."

Seth Livingstone, *USA Today Sports Weekly*

CELEBRATING THE REDS' STORIED HISTORY

Like all ballparks designed for the 21ˢᵗ century, the Great American Ball Park is a rich mixture of the old and new—Cincinnati's past and present. Hoping to capture the Reds' storied past from Crosley Field and winning tradition at Riverfront Stadium, the Great American Ball Park embodies all that the players and fans alike would want in a modern baseball facility. Seth Livingstone's piece about all things Great American was published in the April 2–8, 2003, issue of USA Today Sports Weekly.

Entering his 52ⁿᵈ season in the Reds' organization, Joe Nuxhall has sauntered into more than his share of great American ballparks, but the old left-hander was bowled over when he entered the not-quite-complete Great American Ball Park for the first time.

"You know that this is a *baseball* stadium," said the Reds' longtime broadcaster. "Old Crosley [Field], that was a relic. At the time we moved into Riverfront [1970], that was a state-of-the-art, multipurpose stadium. But you can tell this is strictly baseball. Inside, it's a lot nicer than I expected."

Nuxhall, who made his debut on the mound in 1944 at the tender age of 15, is part of Reds folklore. As he walked out of the Reds' offices and strolled through the Crosley Terrace—a garden area to be dotted with bronze statues of players past (including his own)—his breath was taken away by the nostalgia, then the view.

"From almost directly behind home plate, you look out over the right-field fence, across the river, and see Kentucky," marveled Nuxhall. "Then you look to left field and you see the huge scoreboard above the bleachers—and it is huge."

There's a lot of history to savor at Great American Ball Park, from mosaics depicting the original 1869 Cincinnati Red Stockings and 1975 Big Red Machine to banners commemorating significant events in franchise history to the replica Longines clock that became a Crosley Field landmark.

"What reminds me most of Crosley is the right-field bleachers," Nuxhall said. "They were called the 'Sun Deck' during the day and the 'Moon Deck' at night. If it was a night game, you could see the moon shining. Left field was the sun field. Those right-field bleachers at Great American look like that."

Chief operating officer John Allen says he feels like a "proud father" after nurturing the Great American project for nearly eight years. He believes the Reds got things right.

"The two things we were trying to achieve in the overall perspective of the project were intimacy and character, and I truly believe we accomplished that," Allen said.

Allen takes special delight in a particular spot not far from his office in the adjacent administration building.

"That's my favorite spot—the Spirit of Baseball relief carving that's 20 feet wide by 50 feet high at the west end of the administration building," he says. "It's depicting a young child looking up at three adult baseball players and in the background are key landmarks of Cincinnati. When you want to have your picture taken with your buddies, this is where you'll go. You'll say, 'Meet you under the Spirit of Baseball Relief near the main entrance.' It's a real picture postcard spot."

Great American is open-air, offering views of the river and downtown as well as easy accessibility to the city. In this case, those heading to the stadium on Sycamore Street can catch a glimpse into the park—just as players will be able to gaze out on the Queen City via a unique arch known as "the notch" or "the gap" on the third-base side.

"Another thing that's pretty unique," says Allen, "is that the cheaper the ticket, the better the view. It truly is the case on the river. You'll see a lot of river traffic, then look out on northern Kentucky and the beautiful, massive Roebling Bridge."

Within the confines, there are plenty of creature comforts beyond the sea of red seats (each of which has its own cup holder). But what fans should appreciate most is the closeness to the game—an intimacy that Allen hopes will restore a "home-field advantage" in Cincinnati.

"In the new ballpark, fans in the front row will be three inches below the playing surface. In the old park, they were four and a half to five feet above it," Allen said. "Fans are going to feel like they're part of the action, and that's something we didn't have at Riverfront/Cinergy."

Cincinnati players should feel at home in the expansive clubhouse trimmed in (what else?) red and light wood. The huge "C" in the carpet is a virtual reflection of the "C" that dominates the ceiling above.

"Walking through there, I had this giddy feeling," said infielder Aaron Boone, who toured the facility in January before heading to spring training.

"Maybe that's why spring training seems to have gone by so quickly—because we have something new to look forward to," pitcher

Danny Graves said. "It's like moving into a new house...having 16 TVs instead of three—that's something everybody's looking forward to."

"I was very impressed with the clubhouse—just the dimensions of it," said Nuxhall, who retired as a player in 1967. "Each locker has its own electrical outlet. There are TVs in the middle of the room and that big red "C" in the ceiling. The training room was huge. The whirlpool looks like a swimming pool. And the batting cages are right there, outside the clubhouse."

Although the structure of Great American Ball Park is primarily painted steel, the exterior features a brick façade with a cast stone base. Designed by HOK Sport of Kansas City and GBBN Architects of Cincinnati, it was built by Hunt Construction Group of Indianapolis.

In March 1996, Cincinnati voters approved a half-cent hike in sales tax to fund an estimated $544 million for new stadiums for the Bengals and Reds. The cost of the football stadium, however, exceeded the original estimate for both facilities. In November 1998, voters finally approved building a baseball park on the riverfront, while ruling out a popular Broadway Commons plan.

Groundbreaking for the ballpark, situated between Firstar Center and Cinergy Field, took place October 4, 2000. Cinergy Field was demolished by implosion last December.

In July 2000, Great American Insurance bought 30 years' worth of naming rights for $75 million. It so happens that Great American Insurance, like the Reds, is controlled by billionaire Carl Lindner.

Tickets have sold well for the first season. Luxury suites sold out in 37 days.

Historical Elements

Nearly two-thirds of the fans entering Great American Ball Park will do so by strolling through Crosley Terrace, a 50,000-square-foot tribute to the Reds' home from 1934 to 1969. Designed as a mock infield, it will include tributes to former stars Frank Robinson, Ernie Lombardi, Ted Kluszewski, and Joe Nuxhall in the form of bronze statues. The frame of the planters will double as benches and are inscribed with stories about memorable moments from the Crosley Field era.

In addition to Italian marble mosaics depicting the original 1969 Cincinnati Red Stockings and the 1975 World Series champs, banners commemorating dates in team history grace the walkways inside and out. Along Second Street, banners will commemorate the Reds' first world championship in 1919 and Rose's record-breaking hit. Another set of banners will hang within Crosley Terrace, paying tribute to such events as baseball's first night game in 1935 and Johnny Vander Meer's consecutive no-hitters in 1938.

On the façade beneath the press box will hang the team's six retired numbers: 1 (Fred Hutchinson), 5 (Johnny Bench), 8 (Joe Morgan), 18 (Kluszewski), 20 (Robinson), and 24 (Tony Perez).

The Reds Hall of Fame and Museum will be located just west of the ballpark, located on the site formerly occupied by Riverfront Stadium/Cinergy Field. It's slated to open in 2004 and will feature permanent and traveling exhibits and be open to the public year-round.

To say the Reds never promised fans a Rose Garden would be completely untrue. A Rose Garden, in tribute to Pete Rose, will be located on the site where Rose's 4,192nd hit landed September 11, 1985. The spot, south of the Reds Hall of Fame, is expected to be dedicated in 2004.

The back of the left-field scoreboard, visible from the river, features a massive picture of the bat and ball Rose used to break Ty Cobb's hit record.

Playing Surface

The grass at Great American Ball Park is comprised of five varieties of Kentucky bluegrass, custom-grown for the Reds in Brookville, Indiana. The turf is growing in a foot-deep root zone, composed of sand. The drainage and irrigation systems lay below the root zone. The Reds say the field—with more than two miles of pipe beneath four inches of gravel and 6,000 tons of sand—can handle up to three inches of rain in an hour with little to no water pooling on the surface.

The Ohio dirt mix infield is comprised of the same dirt the Cleveland Indians are using at Jacobs Field. Home plate is 580 feet from the Ohio River. After the final game at Crosley Field, the plate was dug up and flown by helicopter to Riverfront Stadium, where it was used until 1997. The replacement plate was dug up and transported to Great American Ball Park after the final game at Cinergy Field last September 22.

Foul territory in Cincinnati has been significantly reduced, but the new ballpark retains historic dimensions. It's 328 feet to the 12-foot wall in left field, the same as it was at Crosley Field. It's 404 feet to the eight-foot wall in center field, the same as it was at Riverfront/Cinergy. The eight-foot wall in right is only 325 feet from home plate.

Safety

Crosley Field was under 21 feet of water in 1937, and Riverfront Stadium was under 10 feet thanks to flooding in 1997. Learning from history, Cincinnati has installed a solid flood wall to keep back the Ohio River.

In partnership with the U.S. Coast Guard, the Reds have installed a "repeater" in the outfield wall. Radio signals bounce off it to a transmitter around the bends in the river, enabling barges, riverboats, and recreation traffic to receive and transmit.

Great American Ball Park is equipped with a state-of-the-art weather tracking system (NEXRAD, or Next Generation Radar), which can determine the path of storms and warn team officials of potentially dangerous weather systems in advance of their arrival.

The park is also equipped with an anti-lightning system known as the Prevection 4 E.A.S.E. (Electronically Activated Streamer Emission) Air Terminal System. The system intercepts and controls potential strikes, using the park's light towers to grab and store atmospheric energy and carry it safely to the ground.

Seating

Fans will be closer to the action. On the first-base side, the distance from the first row of the upper deck to home plate is 163 feet, two inches (compared to 185 feet at Cinergy Field). The distance from the last row is 259 feet, seven inches (compared to 280 feet). It's a similar story on the third-base side, where the comparisons are even more favorable to the new ballpark.

Fans can enter Great American Ball Park for as little as $5 for seats on the outer view level. The outer view seats offer panoramic vistas of the Ohio River, downtown Cincinnati, Mount Adams, and northern Kentucky.

Seats in the double-decked bleachers, located under the main scoreboard in left field, will sell for $10. Bleacher patrons will have their own beer garden.

The most exclusive seats in the house—the first eight rows directly behind home plate—are called the Diamond Seats and are reserved for season-ticket holders. Fans will pay $175–$210 for wider, upholstered seats as well as complimentary food, beverages, and parking. Access to the private Diamond Lounge is another perk.

Considered one of the architectural highlights of Great American is the Batter's Eye Pavilion, a glass-enclosed, climate-controlled function area in center field. The party area can accommodate 100–170 fans, who receive a catered buffet along with their game ticket for $70. Smaller party suites are also available, as is a 102-seat Party Deck in right field and the RedLegs Landing patio party area.

Of the ballpark's 42,463 seats, approximately 20,000 are on the field level (compared to roughly 10,000 of the 52,000 seats at Cinergy). Those with premium seats will enjoy padded chair cushions and the ability to order food and beverages without leaving their seat, in addition to the best sight lines in the house.

Behind the Diamond Seats are the padded Scout Seats, which sell for $60 and feature in-seat food and beverage service, access to private restroom areas, and access to the Fox Sports Net Club 4192.

Fans sitting in the upper levels will have an unobstructed view of the action thanks to glass railings. Every seat has been oriented toward home plate and each has a cup holder. Smoking is prohibited in all seating areas.

For the Players

Right down to heated dugout seats and private indoor running tracks, Great American Ball Park provides a major upgrade for players.

For one thing, they'll have more space with larger lockers and larger training facilities. In the clubhouse, each player will have an Ethernet connection at his locker and access to a dining room, lounge, and kitchen area.

The Reds have their own video-replay room, weight room, and chapel. Training facilities include a submersible treadmill and conditioning whirlpool.

The dugouts, easily accessible from the home and visitors clubhouses, offer clear views of the playing field. The Reds' bullpen is located in center field, next to the Batter's Eye Pavilion. The visitors' bullpen is in right field, next to the Sun/Moon Deck, and is visible from the outfield concourse.

Entertainment

When a Reds player homers or a Reds pitcher records the game's final out, expect the Pepsi Power Stacks to fire up. This riverboat-inspired celebration machine features mock smoke stacks, LED video panels, fireworks, and a cooling mist. The 64-foot stacks are located between the Sun/Moon Deck and the Batter's Eye Pavilion.

Team mascot Mr. Red now resides at Great American Ball Park and can be spotted in the stands and atop the dugouts. He will be joined by Gapper, his new shaggy red sidekick.

The Pepsi Red Rally Pack—a troupe of performers whose function is to generate crowd energy and enthusiasm—will be back.

Aesthetics

They call it "the Gap."

It's the opening along the third-base side of the stadium that provides spectacular views of downtown Cincinnati. It also permits motorists and pedestrians heading south on Sycamore Street to peek at the action inside Great American Ball Park.

Left field is dominated by the main scoreboard, 68 feet tall and nearly 218 feet wide. Atop the scoreboard will sit the larger-than-original replica of Crosley's Longines clock.

The video board, adjacent to the main scoreboard, offers 68 billion (we wonder who's counting) shades of color on a 27' x 49 3/4' high-definition screen.

Fan Services/Amenities

Fans should appreciate the central concourse, particularly on rainy days. It's large enough to protect all patrons during inclement weather.

Fans will ride three escalators (the longest of which, at 125 feet long, is the longest in the Ohio/Kentucky/Indiana area) to upper-level seats. The park also boasts 14 elevators, 12 more than at Cinergy Field.

In addition to the 28 concession stands, Great American Ball Park provides 29 public restrooms and 531 public toilets. All restrooms feature diaper-changing stations and handicap accessibility. The stadium has 27 ticket windows, four first-aid stations, and fan accommodation stations on the Terrace and View levels.

To keep fans up to date, the out-of-town scoreboard is located in the left-field wall. Along the first- and third-base lines are LED ribbon boards that offer promotional information and personalized messages.

Those leaving their seats won't have to worry about missing the action, as 565 television sets have been installed to handle the in-park game feed.

The Reds estimate they control more than 3,500 parking spots within six blocks of the stadium. That includes 600 spots beneath the park—a number that will expand to roughly 1,000 by 2004. In addition to local bus service, a water taxi services the area from northern Kentucky.

NOTES

The publisher has made every effort to determine the copyright holder for each piece in *Echoes of Cincinnati Reds*.

Reprinted courtesy of *Baseball Magazine*: "Four Hundred to One" (no byline), copyright © September, 1915; "How the New World's Championship Was Won" by W.A. Phelon, copyright © December, 1919; "Editorial Comment" (no byline), copyright © December, 1919; "Eppa, Not Jeptha, Rixey—A Colorful Southpaw" by F.C. Lane, copyright © February, 1930; "Derringer and Wilson Heroes" by Daniel M. Daniel, copyright © November, 1940.

Reprinted with permission of the *Chicago Tribune*: "Reds Find that Piniella's Way Works" by Fred Mitchell, copyright © June 24, 1990.

Reprinted courtesy of the *Cincinnati Enquirer*: "Reds Are World Champions" by Jack Cronin and Lou Smith, copyright © Oct. 9, 1940; " 'Sparky Who' Showed Them" by Jim Schottelkotte, copyright © 1976; "Palace of the Fans" by John Erardi, copyright © April 1, 1996; "Come Full Circle" by John Erardi, copyright © June 26, 2002.

Reprinted courtesy of the *Cincinnati Post*: "Vander Meer on Pinnacle" by Stanley Frank, copyright © June 16, 1938.

Reprinted courtesy of *Cincinnati Times-Star*: "Pat Moran—A Foch of Managers" by James Isaminger, copyright © March 7, 1924.

Reprinted courtesy of the *Cincinnati Times-Star, Cincinnati Enquirer* and *Cincinnati Post*: "Dedication of the Palace of the Fans Grandstand Souvenir Program," copyright © April 17, 1902.